For additional material and photos,
please visit NoOrdinaryBoy.com

❖ ❖ ❖

# No Ordinary Boy
## The Life and Death of Owen Turney

Jennifer Johannesen

low to the ground
PUBLISHING

Copyright © 2011 Jennifer Johannesen

All rights reserved under International and Pan-American Copyright Conventions. No part of this book may be reproduced in any form or by any electronic or mechanical means, including information storage and retrieval systems, without permission in writing from the publisher, except by a reviewer, who may quote brief passages in a review.

Published in Canada by Low to the Ground Publishing, a division of Low to the Ground Consulting Inc., Toronto, 2011.

This book is not intended as a substitute for the medical advice of physicians and/or other healthcare practitioners.

Library and Archives Canada Cataloguing in Publication

Johannesen, Jennifer
No ordinary boy : the life and death of Owen Turney / Jennifer Johannesen.

ISBN 978-0-9877367-0-3

1. Johannesen, Jennifer--Family. 2. Turney, Owen. 3. Parents of children with disabilities--Canada--Biography. 4. Children with disabilities--Canada. I. Title.

HQ759.913.J64 2011     649'.151     C2011-906265-8

Interior book design by Natalia Pérez Wahlberg

Printed and bound in the United States of America

10  9  8  7  6  5  4  3  2  1

**For Angus**
—  —

# Foreword

As Owen's physician and healthcare advisor, I have known Owen and his family for many years, witnessing first-hand several of the events that Owen's mother Jennifer writes about in *No Ordinary Boy*.

Although Owen was profoundly physically and developmentally challenged, I came to appreciate the fullness of his life, the richness of his experiences and the value of his home-based education—all of which seemed to bring joy to Owen and those who cared for him. His smile and playful demeanour spoke volumes. I believe that his life, though short, was rich and meaningful.

Jennifer's account of their journey through the labyrinths of healthcare institutions and education programs reminds me that there is more to a family's journey than what appears in the clinical setting—the decision-making and emotional processing that Jennifer so candidly describes. It has been a privilege to see, from Jennifer's perspective, a side of this family's life I had previously not been exposed to.

*No Ordinary Boy* is a must read for all health professionals as it provides important insights into the context of family-centred care, and allows us to more fully appreciate our patients' experiences and concerns. Ultimately, the book reminds us why we do what we do—and inspires us to do better.

**Dr. Golda Milo-Manson, MD, FRCPC**
Vice-President Medicine and Academic Affairs, Holland Bloorview Kids Rehabilitation Hospital; Associate Professor, Department of Paediatrics, University of Toronto
September, 2011

# Preface

My son Owen was born in August 1998 with severe, multiple disabilities that remained undiagnosed until his death at the age of twelve, in October 2010.

Before Owen's death, I had planned to write a guidebook — an *Advocacy for Dummies* sort of book. I started the project many times, each effort ending in frustration. I eventually realized: I have no universal advice to give. No tips or tricks. My successes and failures in advocating for and raising Owen were largely dictated by my surroundings, my experience and my personality. How could I recommend anything to someone who might have an entirely different world view? Or who might live in a small town instead of a large metropolitan city? Or who might have six other children to care for as well? If I wrote a guidebook, I thought, it would be relevant only to people exactly like me.

I had almost abandoned the idea of a book when Owen suddenly, inexplicably, died. I was in shock. I hibernated for the three months immediately following his death, finding refuge on my couch, closing myself off to the world. Eventually, I felt the impulse to write again and spent the next several months exploring my writing "voice" and seeking out the story I wanted to share. This book is the result of that exploration.

Throughout the book, I return to certain moments in my journey as Owen's main advocate and, of course, as his mother. I describe the often absurd, sometimes harrowing situations I encountered in caring for Owen (particularly when engaging with medical, educational and rehabilitative institutions) and the decision-making processes required in doing so. Although readers may find some of the anecdotes useful, this book offers little explicit advice. Instead, the stories illuminate the ethical and emotional challenges of caring for one so deeply vulnerable and dependent.

I suspect different types of readers will each come away from this book with something different. For example, medical and educational professionals may find themselves reflecting on their own practices, how they engage with patients and how they present their knowledge and employ their expertise. Parents and caregivers of children with disabilities may see a reflection, a mirror in which they are reminded of their own experiences, and may come to a deeper understanding of their fears and personal motivations. Yet others may have no connection to the subject matter but recognize the complexity of decision-making in a vast sea of options with unpredictable outcomes.

However you relate to this story, my hope is that one message stands out clearly: the more options we have when seeking to improve the quality of a life, the more carefully we must take each into account.

# One

On family history, Owen's mother is 27 years old and healthy. She has beta thalassemia trait. Owen's father is 34 years old and healthy. Owen has a 4-year-old half-brother who is also healthy. Owen's mother is of Norwegian and Chinese descent, and his father is of English and Dutch descent. Owen's parents are non-consanguineous. The maternal family history reveals a number of people with macular degeneration, uterine cancer, breast cancer and other cancers. There is no family history of congenital abnormalities or recurrent spontaneous abortions. There is no history of hearing loss, muscle weakness, seizures, kidney failure, diabetes or stroke.

**The Hospital for Sick Children, Division of Clinical and Metabolic Genetics, February 17, 2000**

I can't remember the first midwife's name. Might have been Andrea. The Midwife Collective model meant that I had a main midwife and then a back-up midwife—I would see one person consistently and at some point further in the pregnancy get acquainted with another. Of course midwives have more than one client at a time and are always on call, and this system helps ensure that babies will be delivered by a midwife with whom the mother is familiar.

My last appointment with the Collective (although I didn't know it was to be my last) was with Sarilyn. She was filling in for someone else, who I think was to be my secondary midwife. So the back-fill was replacing the backup. Sarilyn was old school—a funky grandma who had been delivering babies for a while. Kind and thorough, and a bit of a hippie.

I was expecting the usual appointment—urine sample, weigh and measure, chit-chat. I was 28 weeks pregnant and had been following along with the *What to Expect When You're Expecting Book* with religious fervour. I knew that this particular time of the pregnancy, 28 weeks, was a bit of a dead zone in the check-ups. Hold the course, keep steady with activities, yes you can eat what you want . . . No preparations yet, no birth ritual discussions. I felt I knew what to expect, which was not much.

One thing did bother me slightly. I wondered about some tension I'd been feeling across my abdomen. My belly had become barrel-like—not a low-down rounded bump most women have at this point, but a high-up thickness that didn't vary from top to bottom. My whole torso felt tight and sore. My skin was stretched uncomfortably and I found it difficult to breathe, especially when I was seated.

I was bothered by it but told myself that my symptoms didn't seem unusual—any number of indignities can be experienced at this stage and it wasn't unreasonable to think I was just getting a bum deal. I mentioned to Sarilyn that everything was more or less fine—I was getting sleep, eating okay, feeling energetic—just one little thing was bugging me, and it was that I felt really pregnant! We laughed and moved on to the physical exam.

Part of the pregnancy assessment is to measure the belly, to compare it against average growth (number of inches roughly equals number of weeks gestation), and to compare it against the previous month's measurement. Given both of these sets of numbers, at 28 weeks I should have measured 28 to 30 inches.

Sarilyn tried to wrap the tape measure around me but I was too big to reach around. She tried to toss it around and catch it with her other hand—no luck. I passed the end around myself, enabling her to bring the ends of tape the together to find the reading.

We both saw the measurement at the same time: *44 inches.*

Sarilyn put down the measuring tape and said the number out loud.

I thought, "Well, that explains why I'm so uncomfortable."

❖ ❖ ❖ ❖ ❖

Twins or diabetes. Those were the "good" options—one was good because it was a normal anomaly, and the other because it was a known and treatable condition.

"There are other reasons you might be so large," Sarilyn said, "but let's not talk about those unless we have to."

I could hear the uncertainty in her voice—part fear, part lack of medical experience with such things. I had no frame of reference; the *What to Expect* book didn't have a section about this. I only understood that if it was not twins or diabetes, things might be very, very bad.

❖ ❖ ❖ ❖ ❖

I had, all along, resisted "medicalizing" my pregnancy. I had opted out of any prenatal testing and ultrasounds—there was no history of physical or developmental issues in my family and I was perfectly healthy, so no intrusions or sneak-peeks necessary.

This was all about to change. Sarilyn suggested, then insisted, that an ultrasound was required to clear up the mystery. I obliged with little fuss, surprising myself with how easily I agreed.

I opened my appointment book to explore dates for the following week. Let's see . . . meetings Monday, maybe can squeeze in Tuesday, Wednesday is free, Thursday I'm—

My thoughts were interrupted.

"Actually, I was thinking now."

I looked up from my book. "Pardon?"

"I mean now. Right now."

# Two

I drove myself from Sarilyn's office in the east end of Toronto to the ultrasound clinic downtown. I was a little worried, a little excited, and was happy to skip out on work for the next couple of hours. I circled the block a few times looking for parking, deciding in the end to park in the public garage, making a mental note to get to a bank machine to pay my way out.

The clinic had its own storefront space in an office building across from Women's College, a well-known hospital specializing in women's health. The waiting room felt like a holding pen for a casting call: "Pregnant Woman, Frazzled." No seats. I checked in with the receptionist then stood in the corner waiting for my name to be called.

I don't remember feeling anxious—I was excited that I was going to see my baby! Declining the opportunity for prior testing meant giving up an ultrasound picture on the fridge and not knowing the sex of the baby. Now, ordered to have an ultrasound for Serious Medical Purposes I could, indeed, take a peek.

I was surprised to be called almost immediately. I suppose Sarilyn impressed upon them that I was an emergency case although I am quite sure I didn't look like one yet. And I certainly didn't know it.

❖ ❖ ❖ ❖ ❖

I lay on the table dutifully as the soft-spoken technician did the scan. The cold gel felt smooth and weird as she guided the roller across my belly. It was painful—she pressed, rolled and jammed the wand into whatever softer pockets she could find around the sides of my belly. I noticed she was returning to certain spots over and over again.

When she started speaking, I was surprised to hear her voice because I knew she wasn't talking to me. She was in fact speaking to the ultrasound machine—muttering measurements, anatomical bits and noteworthy findings into the microphone; recording audio and video to review later with the radiologist.

I wondered, as I lay there, if I ought to ask the technician what was going on or if I should just lie quietly and wait until she was done. I decided that it was best not to interrupt, that she probably wouldn't share anything with me anyway. I tried to look at the monitor during the ultrasound process but between the poor angles, bad lighting and the technician subtly nudging the tilt of the monitor away from me, I couldn't make out what was going on. Not that I would have understood what I was looking at.

The technician got up abruptly after many minutes and fetched the radiologist, a woman who barely said hello and made a beeline for the monitor to watch the recorded film. She leaned closely into the screen, her face radiating reflected light, eyes tight with concentration, eyeglasses pushed up onto the top of her head. The technician hovered behind her and stooped in, pointing to this and that while the radiologist nodded. After an excruciating number of minutes, they both stood up—the technician slunk back towards the drawn curtain behind her, the radiologist straightened her back and gazed at me steadily.

In hindsight, I think this was the moment. This was the moment I knew life was about to change and I barely had time to brace myself. I was eager—desperate—for her to speak to me but also didn't want what might be coming. For the first time it occurred to me to make a wish: please just tell me the baby is alive.

"Who is your doctor?"

"I don't have a doctor. I have a midwife."

Pause. "You will need to talk to her. I will write the report and then you will need to go see her. You will have some decisions to make."

Silence.

I wanted to ask more, demand to know what was going on, insist on knowing it all, right then and there. But it was awkward. I was still lying on the table with my belly exposed, the baby pressing on my bladder and my skin wet and cold from the gel. I struggled to get up—much like an elephant does—in stages. Instead of front leg, front leg, back leg, back leg, it was roll on side, press with hands, one leg swings down, other leg down, reorient from dizziness . . .

By the time I was upright both women were gone.

❖ ❖ ❖ ❖ ❖

I came out to the reception area, disoriented and confused.

Everything was fine when I first entered the waiting room and now everything was not. Although nothing had actually changed, everything now looked different. I tried to reassure myself that the only difference was the information about something or other that was happening anyway, whether I initially knew about it or not. Whether I liked it or not. This was an earnest but doomed tactic—I'm sure that to the other patients I looked panicked and wild-eyed. There was still no available seat so I stood in a back corner, waiting for the promised report.

About ten minutes later, the receptionist summoned me over and handed me an envelope. It was letter-sized, dark yellow. Sealed.

She said quietly, "Give this to your doctor."

I stood there staring at it, holding it in my hand. It didn't occur to me to rip it open—after all, it wasn't addressed to me. Instead, I decided to phone my midwife. The clinic personnel gave me little direction or guidance and I thought perhaps Sarilyn would know what to do next. If nothing else, I had this envelope to give her... I opened my phone to see that the battery had died. Now what should I do?

The clinic was exceptionally busy, and there were many women and couples sitting and standing around. Perhaps I should ask to borrow someone's cellphone. I searched the faces and no one made eye contact with me, although I had felt conspicuous and closely observed when I came back to the reception area after my ultrasound. I'm guessing all the women felt this way. On one hand, there's a feeling of community and affinity; on the other hand, a bitchy wariness. Do I look like that? I don't look like that... She's really heavy and tired... I hope I don't look like that! So, no, I didn't borrow a phone.

The only other potential phone was the receptionist's, which was in use and located rather inconveniently from where I stood, under the top overhang of the façade of the desk. No matter—I must speak with Sarilyn. I asked to use the phone.

The curly phone cord was quite short. In order to speak into the mouthpiece and also have the receiver to my ear, I had to extend the cord taut, stand on tiptoes and try not to fall over or sweep everything off the desk. My part of the conversation was audible to all.

Sarilyn answered on the first ring. She suggested I come back to her office to discuss what was happening. She wasn't sure how she was going to advise me yet but we would need to meet, review the report, make decisions. Again, the word "decisions."

I said, "I don't know what is going on. Decisions about what?"

I braced myself, told myself at that moment that whatever she says, it will be okay. All my esoteric new-momma rules had already flown out the window. I would take any medications, endure any radiation, drink any potions, do whatever I needed to do to make this right.

Sarilyn responded: "Decide whether or not to terminate the pregnancy."

Terminate? I was seven months pregnant.

I hung up the phone, in shock and hyper-alert. Okay, what next? Get the car, call Michael, go to Sarilyn's. I'll fetch Michael on the way. Michael! He doesn't know! Wait, where's the car? Parking garage! I have no cash with me.

It was hard to see as I tried to sort things out through a wall of tears. Bank machine, parking garage, navigate traffic. Thankfully, a straight drive across Gerrard Street to my house across town.

As I sat at a traffic light I was so overcome by panic that I forgot I was pregnant. I forgot I had just been told we might have to abort our 7-month-old unborn child. I forgot there was a mystery unfolding that no one would reveal to me. I could only think of one thing at a time, and my current task was to just get home.

I then noticed the envelope on the passenger's seat. I must have tossed it there when I got into the car. Right, I remember now. I hesitated, then ripped it open.

It contained a single piece of paper—a form that had the proverbial scrawled handwriting of a harried doctor in a busy clinic. Measurements, arrows, technical information, finally an opinion:

*Hydrops fetalis.* Prognosis guarded.

❖ ❖ ❖ ❖ ❖

Michael had been expecting me when I arrived home. On most days, he worked from home, in his upstairs office. Sarilyn must have called him. He heard me come in and scrambled, alarmed and concerned, down the front stairs.

When I saw Michael, I collapsed. We huddled on the stairs as I tried to relay what happened, and he tried to absorb things as quickly as he could. There was urgency in the air.

In the meantime, Sarilyn had done her homework. She knew this hydrops (whatever it is) was outside the scope of what she was contracted to do: deliver a healthy baby to a healthy mother. Instead of meeting at the midwives' office, we agreed we would meet at the Mount Sinai Hospital High Risk Pregnancy Clinic. I knew nothing of the facility or the clinic.

Sarilyn, through experience or instinct, knew it was the right place and had made only the one phone call. Her decision to take us to Mount Sinai saved Owen's life.

# Three

The first few hours at the hospital were a haze of countless ultrasounds and a parade of physicians. The doctors were impressed with the radiologist's best guess. In the end, the initial diagnosis was correct. Indeed, Owen had hydrops fetalis—an accumulation of fluid in his chest, abdomen and other parts, symptomatic of a number of conditions and illnesses. The cause of Owen's hydrops would remain a mystery for the rest of his life.

This was clearly a fascinating case. Some of the doctors were called in, not for their opinions, but rather to see this rare and interesting anomaly. I didn't mind that we'd become celebrities; I gleaned much from their candid conversations with each other. But I learned much more when Dr. Ryan sat us down to have The Talk.

He didn't pull any punches. Owen was filling with fluid. This was no standard-issue swelling. Rather, his abdomen and chest cavities were blowing up like balloons. In place of air, amniotic fluid. If left unattended, he—we'd just learned our baby was a boy, not a girl as we had guessed—would likely die in utero, or put my body under such stress that I would go into premature labour.

To make sure we understood the severity of the condition, Dr. Ryan showed us the ultrasound pictures of Owen floating in a vast ocean of fluid, his organs floating in his body like planets in the void of outer space. When I googled *hydrops fetalis* later, I found images of monstrously bloated fetuses.

Owen's scrotum was swollen round and taut, his tiny testicles lost in the expanse of the sac. The link between the torso and the scrotum had not yet sealed itself (premature boys often require inguinal hernia repair about a year after they are born) so the fluid was free to travel wherever there was easy passage. He looked extraterrestrial—short stubby arms, tiny dangling legs spread apart by a weirdly enlarged scrotal sac, huge head, round belly. (I thought, though, that he was beautiful—a good thing because Owen looked this way for many years to come. My adoration never waned.)

Dr. Ryan spoke calmly, ensuring that we understood at every step what he was saying. The fluid was not processing in and out of the fetus, as it should. Owen was filling up, and so was I. Both of us were reaching capacity and bad things would happen if we did not drain the fluid.

I wondered out loud, "So maybe it's not so bad for me to go into labour. Get Owen out where we can treat him."

I was disabused of this notion quickly; not only do babies need to stay in the womb as long as possible for their development, but it was now risky for me to go into labour. Owen was so big that at 28 weeks he had exceeded the size of a full-term baby—perhaps not in height but certainly in girth. If I were to try to deliver him vaginally, he might get stuck. Really stuck. If you dare to imagine that, you can imagine how things could get ugly.

The only answer was to drain the fluid from both of us. Using ultrasound as a guide, a pigtail shunt would be inserted into Owen's body to continue the drainage.

"But, how will you get it in?" I was not a little horrified but I was genuinely curious.

The answer was distressing: a long, sharp-ended straw will be inserted through the skin of my belly, through the muscle wall and through the lining of the uterus, eventually making its way to a position just outside of Owen's chest. Internal pressure will force some of the fluid out through the straw. The shunt, usually coiled (like a pig's tail) but pliable enough to be straightened, will be guided down through the tube and out the other end, eventually puncturing Owen's body and resting with one end inside the fluid-filled cavity of his chest and the other end open to the amniotic sac, outside of Owen's body. The outer straw will then be withdrawn, leaving the shunt inside, re-coiled and secure.

I don't remember reacting emotionally. I recall that I sat there, poised and collected, mind swirling with the images of what I thought this would all look like, staring down the inevitable path I knew I must take.

"Let's do it."

Dr. Ryan looked at me. "Well, there's one more thing . . ."

The accumulation of extra fluid throughout Owen's body meant that the visual symptoms of other underlying syndromes or challenges were obscured. Typical prenatal testing at this point would have included chromosome testing to reveal conditions such as Down syndrome, or other development anomalies like spina bifida. I had so far opted not to have any prenatal testing done, so none of these had been ruled out or in. One indication of Down syndrome in particular is excess fat at the back of the neck. Owen's shape was so distorted there was no possible way of taking definitive measurements.

We were invited to consider chromosome testing before intervening and to postpone treatment of our dying baby so that we could first determine if there was something else wrong with him. Was this purely for medical reasons? Perhaps if he did indeed have Down syndrome, more would be known about, say, his heart, so diagnosis would be more predictive and treatment more effectively suited to his needs.

Or was this suggested because the results would determine if intervention would be "worth it"? Do we want to save an already disabled baby? No one said it, but I wonder now if this was the real underlying question. Is it even fair to dissect this moment, to look back and judge? Wasn't it reasonable to want to know all the facts, using all the tests at our disposal, before moving forward?

"And so . . . ?"

Dr. Ryan was patient but I guess he was waiting for Michael and me to make a decision. Quickly.

❖ ❖ ❖ ❖ ❖

I was reminded that this was the front end of a long weekend. Any samples would need to be sent away now before the labs closed. Preliminary results would be ready as early as next week. Michael and I deliberated between ourselves: there are good reasons to wait. We've made it this far, we can last three more days. It would be bad if something happened on the weekend. Best to know all knowable facts. Reasonable enough, yes?

I spoke for both of us. "We'll test. Test, get the results and then decide."

Yes, test and then decide. But wait a second . . . decide what? My brain was already full but I had to squeeze in a bit more:

"So, what if next week we decide to abort? Or what if he doesn't survive the procedure?"

A C-section perhaps? And how does one abort a third-trimester baby anyway? I already knew that regardless of the test results I would not pursue an abortion. But I just had to talk through all possible scenarios.

"Ontario doesn't allow third-trimester abortions. But there is a clinic in the U.S. It will cost $10,000 but they would do it right away." My stomach stirred. I felt nauseous for the first time in my pregnancy.

"And if the baby dies during the procedure, we would induce labour."

"Labour? You don't just . . . you know . . . take it out?"

"No. We would give you medication and after a few days you would deliver the body." Nausea turned to dizziness.

"The baby would be dead and I would carry it until I expel it?"

"Yes."

"And if I don't get an abortion and we choose not to intervene...?"

"The baby will not likely survive its condition, in which case we will induce and you will deliver the body. If it does survive, the baby will continue to get bigger as it accumulates more fluid, and your body will naturally think it's time to deliver and it's unlikely there's enough room for it to come out. It could be a crisis for both of you."

There were no good options. I can't explain now and I couldn't have explained then, but in that room, at that moment, we decided to perform the tests and wait.

❖ ❖ ❖ ❖ ❖

A full weekend of waiting. I felt on edge, disconnected from the world, hyper-aware of the unwell baby inside me who was also enduring this crisis, even more directly than I. To distract ourselves Michael and I went to an outdoor jazz festival. We sat in the grass, tapped our fingers to the rhythms of the music, pretended we were just a normal young couple expecting our first baby together.

Did we talk? Did we cry? Did we express our fears to each other? I wish I could say "yes" and describe how this crisis brought us together. No. We suffered the crushing wait in silence, each, at times, wondering what the other did to cause this.

What were we to do if the tests came back positive? What was our plan?

I don't know. We didn't talk about it.

❖ ❖ ❖ ❖ ❖

Four days later we got the call. All preliminary results were negative.

Only momentary reprieve, relief from the fear of Door Number Two. No time for celebrations. We must go.

I was lying on a bed in the Case Room that was used for these kinds of less invasive procedures. The whole thing was going to be relatively quick—maybe an hour—and I wasn't going to be under a general anaesthetic. The doctors encouraged me to stay focused, regulate my breathing, tune in to the baby.

The ultrasound machine was directly in front of me so I could watch. I was coached to prepare for discomfort—they could freeze the skin on my belly but there was no way to numb the inside. I would feel the incision, then the insertion of the long straw-like tube through my muscle wall and through my uterus. I would need to breathe calmly, avoid movement, resist distraction. If I felt the fetus move in alarm as the shunt entered its tiny, fragile body, it would be my job to send it calming vibes.

I watched the ultrasound monitor closely along with everyone else. Dr. Ryan was joined by Dr. Windrim, who was going to "drive." Dr. Windrim would insert the shunt and drain the fluid while Dr. Ryan directed the ultrasound angles. It was a bit like working with chopsticks, but only being able to look into a mirror to see what you're doing.

Days earlier, during a conversation with Dr. Ryan: "We will insert the shunt anywhere we can get access, but we have to be careful or we might nick the mum." I thought I misheard.

"You might what?"

"Nick the mum. Cut something we shouldn't. This sort of thing is risky. A mum could die."

These thoughts drifted through my mind as I watched the straw enter, momentarily disassociating what I felt from the image I saw on the monitor. I felt the discomfort of the poke, the sliding, and . . .

look there! On the monitor! There's the baby, lying innocently at the bottom. And there's the bright, white, hard line of the straw pushing down through the layers towards it, a missile launched towards an unsuspecting target. I heard calm voices, felt steady hands—a perfect dance of technology, skill, experience.

I watched the straw jab, then penetrate. Owen jumped, recoiled. Shunt pauses, thrusts. Doctors confer . . . Agreed? Slowly now . . . the pigtail shunt was in.

Sometime during the procedure, fluids from my amniotic sac and from Owen's chest cavity were drained and collected for testing. My belly, now visibly deflated, had become softer again and felt more natural. The incision was barely visible. Someone asked if I wanted a Band-Aid.

But that wasn't the end of it. Fluid would continue to accumulate at a rate faster than the pigtail shunt could channel it out of Owen's body. It was there to provide an open door, a gateway, through which the excess fluid could escape. There would be relief from pressure but that didn't mean there wouldn't eventually be another accumulation—in which case the procedure would be repeated.

Now that Owen had a foreign object lodged in his chest, we both required monitoring, which meant ultrasounds daily, sometimes twice a day. I was focused on staying calm, always walking at a moderate pace, getting lots of rest. I felt huge, and the summer heat didn't help. My ankles and calves had become swollen and spongy. I wore a uniform comprising a tank top under a pair of oversized bib overalls, cut into shorts. I waddled around our neighbourhood in sensible sandals acquired on a recent trip to Amsterdam. I was pleased with my own foresight as I slid those sandals on every day, occasionally having to open them just one more notch. The shunt procedure was repeated a couple of weeks later, resulting in a total of three shunts inserted into Owen—two in his chest and one in his abdomen. On a subsequent occasion, Owen and I were relieved of accumulated fluid. I felt like a water balloon being repeatedly filled and emptied.

The ultrasounds were a confirmation of what I could anticipate hours beforehand. The skin across my belly and lower back would stretch taut and I had terrible heartburn—the baby and fluid were putting too much pressure on my stomach and interfering with digestion. I always knew when I was due for the procedure again.

I had developed a heightened awareness of my baby, and of my body. I slowed way down, stopping frequently to listen, feel, soothe. I can keep this up for ten more weeks, I thought, when my baby reaches full-term and all will be well. How we will look back upon this time and be grateful we made it through!

I was so focused on keeping my baby inside I didn't once think about what would happen when he came out.

# Four

On a warm Saturday evening, four weeks after the first shunt procedure, Michael and I attended a wedding in Kitchener. I wouldn't otherwise have dreamed of attending a social event at this stage but this was family and we thought it was time to get out a bit. I felt the swelling again throughout the evening, the tightness, the cramping, the internal pressure. I told Michael that I wanted to go home.

About twenty minutes into the drive I changed my mind. No, not home. To the hospital.

Oddly, when we arrived at the hospital, they didn't know what to do with me. My own doctors were not on call that night, and the High Risk Clinic took appointments only during regular business hours. We hadn't planned for this to happen in the middle of the night.

Triage nurses spoke with doctors, who spoke with other nurses and front desk clerks. Eventually it was decided that I should stay until Monday, when my doctors would be on shift again and, if needed, someone could be paged to come in the following day. I should at least check myself in and stay in a hospital bed, just in case.

Good thing. Sometime on Sunday afternoon I heaved myself out of bed to use the washroom when my water broke, all over the floor. The attending nurse happened to be in the room. Surely she had seen such things before?

It seems not. She threw some towels on the floor and told me to go back to bed.

"Oh. My. God! Omigod. Good Lord." She was dancing and praying and jumping around—I wondered what the big deal was—I wasn't in labour and I was actually quite happy to have some pressure relieved.

I soon learned that water breakage without labour is not what one wants. The broken sac means that bacteria can enter the birth canal. If the baby would not be coming soon on its own, we would need to encourage it.

A nurse told me to do my breathing. I looked at her blankly. With all of our focus on the pregnancy and keeping the baby in, not only had we not thought about the baby *being out*, we hadn't thought about the baby actually *coming out*. I didn't know the first thing about labour or delivery. My breathing? What does she mean, *my* breathing? I tried to recall movie births—rapid shallow breathing through clenched teeth. Or was it supposed to be deep breathing through an open mouth? Make sounds or hold it in? Push or pull?

For 20 hours I dozed, sweated, grunted, moaned, writhed, cursed, huffed, each hour bringing more intensity and pain. In later conversations I would describe the sensation as the "ring of fire"—a searing and brutal heat wrapped around my body, pressing inward like a vice. The contractions would surge and roar, then throw me down again allowing me to catch my breath, only to start rumbling up again minutes, eventually seconds, later. It was like a roller coaster without the thrill—only dread-filled ascension and terrifying pain. I had no idea it would be like this.

❖ ❖ ❖ ❖ ❖

Michael arrived sometime early in the night, with Justin, Michael's then three-year-old son from his first marriage. He was with us that weekend and, given the late hour, had to come with Michael to the hospital. The best arrangement Michael could make was for Justin to attend daycare early in the morning.

At around 6:00 a.m., Michael took Justin to daycare. At about the same time, probably not coincidentally, I could no longer take the pain. I asked for an epidural. Temporary, barely-there relief. By the time Michael returned I was in full labour.

I was taken to the Case Room for delivery. Only Dr. Ryan, a couple of nurses and Michael were with me. I had no idea that a team of neonatologists was in the next room. I didn't know I was the only one who wasn't preoccupied by the possibility that my baby wouldn't survive. I didn't anticipate that instead of cuddling with me in a soft warm bed, Owen would spend the first hours of his life lying flat on his back on a stainless steel platform in the Resuscitation Room connected to several IVs and a ventilator.

Early in my labour, I asked someone if Owen would be okay.

"Your baby has been through a lot. He might be quite sick."

❖ ❖ ❖ ❖ ❖

The delivery was complicated. Owen became stuck at one point and required suctioning, for which a kind of plunger was stuck to his head so he could be pulled out. Then came an unthinkable order:

"Stop pushing."

They needed to clamp the shunts to reduce the risk of infection. I had to stop breathing in order to stop pushing. My senses closed down; I couldn't see, hear or smell. I thought, "Just please hurry up."

My survival defences must have kicked in. The next few minutes were a haze until—Hallelujah!—a *whoosh* and he was out.

Where is he? I was dying to see him. I imagined a small, pink undersized piglet that I could hold against my skin. I imagined cuddling, soothing. Been through a lot indeed. Where *is* he? I looked around and saw a haze of bodies in white coats. I had removed my glasses during labour and couldn't see anything.

I heard Dr. Ryan say, "No, wait. Let her see him. Quickly."

Let her see him? Of course let her see him! Where are my glasses? Michael was holding them and fumbled to give them to me. A bundle in a blanket was brought over to me—more haze of baby blue (the blanket) and dark purple (the baby). No crying, no fists flailing. What's wrong with him? The bundle was whisked away through a set of adjoining doors and into the next room.

"Where are they taking him?"

"He needs medical attention. He needs resuscitating."

I imagined chest compressions. Mouth to mouth. Turning his tiny body upside down and spanking his bare bottom.

I changed focus as Dr. Ryan surveyed the damage. I would need extensive stitching to repair the tearing. The final stage of the ultimate physical endurance test. It was a small mercy that I didn't know this was really just the beginning of a much bigger one.

❖ ❖ ❖ ❖ ❖

We were brought to a kind of holding room. Michael walked and I was being wheeled. We waited there alone for a long time—easily an hour, maybe two, with no word of our baby or what was going to happen next. No one came to talk to us.

Michael eventually wandered out, looking for someone to give us information. Where is our baby? We wanted to see him. I had accepted as likely that we wouldn't be taking him home that day. That was fine—in all the distraction we hadn't sorted out diapers, the nursery, the crib. Michael could organize things while I recuperated, and we could bring the baby home when he was a bit stronger.

Someone spoke to someone, and a young doctor came to escort us through a series of hallways and "inside" doors—rooms that led to more rooms, giving the sense of an inner sanctum within a greater labyrinth.

Owen was in a small room, laid out on blankets on a metal table. So tiny. Just 5 pounds. Limbs splayed, flat on his back. His abdomen still swollen and distended, his scrotum rounded and puffed out.

His little frog legs were apart, knees turned out, heels almost touching. The dark purple colour was gone and he was now more recognizably flesh-toned. I didn't notice exactly what was sticking out of him where—but he was more or less completely covered in hospital tape and gauze, which fastened various chest tubes, intravenous lines and monitor pads. The ventilator tubing was inserted down through one nostril and aggressively taped to his face. The tape was so tight around his nose his upper lip was distorted into a grimace. His eyes were covered with a soft blindfold to prevent discomfort and damage from the phototherapy lights, used in the treatment of newborn jaundice.

Michael and I stood idiotically, mouths gaping, the doctor standing a short distance away from us, awkward and helpless. I started to cry.

"Can I touch him?"

"Oh! Oh, well, yes, yes of course . . ." Had he never been asked that before?

I approached Owen's tiny self, oblivious to the incessant beeping of the monitors and the pumps, the slow, rhythmic compressions of the ventilator. I extended one finger and gently touched the only part of his body that was not covered with adhesive—a small square of skin on the right side of his belly. Owen's seemingly lifeless body twitched slightly.

The young doctor smiled. "They always know the mum."

❖ ❖ ❖ ❖ ❖

That first day, seeing Owen hooked up to tubes and injected with who-knows-what, gave me a sure sense that he wasn't leaving the hospital any time soon. But no one said so. There was no sit-down. No official here's-what's-wrong-with-your-baby-and-here's-what-we're-going-to-do-about-it. No prognosis, no words of promise or statement of intent. Instead, endless days (which turned to weeks, which turned to months) of moment-to-moment crisis management and speculation. By sometime into the second week of our stay I came to understand through conversations with the nurses that healthy premature babies ("preemies") typically stay in the hospital until their due dates. For Owen, who was not a healthy preemie, it meant he would not be discharged for at least eight weeks. Eight weeks!

I wondered where we would stay—surely parents were allowed to stay with their babies. Could Michael stay too? Would we get our own room? I guess we're moving in!

I was relieved of my naïveté rather quickly. I was to stay in the hospital for just one more day, then return home alone. Owen would be cared for in the Neonatal Intensive Care Unit (NICU) until he was ready for Level 2, where improving babies go before they are released to go home. Of course, they said, I could visit any time.

Once I was assigned my own room on the ward, I asked to see him again.

"He's been moved from the Resuscitation Room. To the NICU."

I was pointed in the general direction, just down the hall, around the corner, down another short hallway with a bleak seating area with photos on the wall of successful "graduates" of intensive care, and through a heavy white door. There was an antechamber with a big trough sink and playfully insistent signs encouraging thorough hand washing. One was especially cheerful, with a cartoon bear and a quote: "Scrubby Bear likes clean hands!" The soap had a harsh anti-bacterial smell, perked up with something floral. Or citrus? Not a smell found in nature. (Later, my brother would say it smelled like corn chips.) A wall phone with a dangling cord hung by a swinging door that opened into the main area. I didn't know that parents were supposed to use the phone to ask permission to come in. I washed my hands as instructed by the sign and walked through the door.

Before visiting for the first time, I thought of the NICU as a high-tech nursery. I imagined sick babies with big round eyes, drinking from bottles that included liquid antibiotics, sleeping in a hushed, carpeted room with fretting mothers at their bedsides, soothing fevers while breastfeeding.

In reality, the room was noisy and chaotic. Painted bright yellow, it was twice the size of a large school classroom with the same kind of flourescent tube lighting. A radio was set to EZ Rock, an adult contemporary music channel, barely audible above the din of the pinging, dinging and clanging of the machinery. Along one wall was a chest-high counter, behind which was the nurses' station. It was a kind of gathering area for staff of all kinds, conferring on cases and completing records.

Bed stations were positioned around the remaining outer walls with more stations located on either side of a single interior wall running through the middle of the room. The room was configured like a running track—you could walk in either direction and end up in the same place.

I didn't see any babies, but I knew they were in their isolettes. Isolettes are transparent, environmentally controlled plexiglass boxes, perfectly sized incubators for tiny preemies and medical apparatus. The beds inside are adjustable so that babies can sleep on an incline to reduce the risk of fluid accumulating in their lungs. All the cables, tubing and monitor leads run into the isolette through apertures in the plexiglass. Doctors and nurses can reach inside to insert an IV, take a baby's temperature or change a diaper through round, hinged windows on either side. Those same hinged windows provide access for parents so they can sit for hours with one hand inside, big finger coaxed into a tiny clenched fist of their doped baby high on morphine to relieve pain and encourage stillness, refusing to withdraw the finger lest the baby wake and find no one there, despite the pressure of the edge of the window against the forearm causing the entire arm to fall asleep and go numb.

Many of the isolettes were covered with blankets to keep out the light. Sometime later a nurse mentioned how covering the isolette helps to replicate the dark in *utero* environment. Right, I think. Sure. As though any of this is at all like being in utero.

The nurse at the desk saw my bewildered look and rumpled hospital gown and didn't need to determine further whether my presence was legitimate. She asked which baby I was there to see, and gently instructed me to use the phone next time. They don't want parents walking in during rounds due to privacy issues—you can't listen in on a report about someone else's baby—and they don't want parents around whose baby is undergoing a procedure. Oftentimes, tests or interventions are performed for which babies remain in their bed stations. It's disruptive and risky to remove them from the NICU, especially as many are on oxygen and in fragile states. Even x-ray machines come to them.

I nodded. "Owen. My baby's name is Owen."

"We go by last name. Mother's last name. Yours is . . . ?"

"Johannesen."

She looked at her notes. "Ah. Baby Johannesen. Bedspace nine." She smiled kindly.

I made my way around the corner to the back wall. The isolette was positioned with the head of the unit close to the wall, the foot of the unit facing into the room. An IV pole supported various pumps that were regulating medications and fluids through the tubes. The ventilator was part of the wall—the outlet for the tubing was just over the bedspace. An accordion-like hollow blue tube was fastened to the outlet and spiraled its way into the isolette. A small desk was attached to the wall and a nurse was standing over it, writing in a binder. I approached and introduced myself.

"Hello," she said. "Just finishing something up and then we'll let you know what's happening."

I sat on a small swivel stool beside the isolette and dared to look inside.

Owen was on his side, no clothes except for the tiniest diaper. The heavy apparatus of the breathing tube seemed to weigh down his whole face, turning his head slightly down towards the blankets. An IV was visible through the skin on his hairless head. Another IV on the back of his hand, held firmly in place with the support of a kind of splint to prevent him from fisting his hand or turning his wrist. As was common practice, the nurse had rigged up a soother—even in extreme distress the reflex to root and suck is strong—using the plunger end of a very large syringe with a feeding nipple stuck onto the end. Owen had found it and was sucking lightly in his sleep. I didn't know what they were, but I counted at least 6 leads that were attached to sticker-like pads scattered on his body, attached to various beeping monitors noting respiration rate, heart rate, oxygen saturation and anything else they could think of to monitor.

❖ ❖ ❖ ❖ ❖

Owen was ten days old before I was allowed to hold him. Although the chest tubes had been removed, he was still connected to the ventilator. The IVs and monitor leads were also still attached to various parts of his body. Lifting Owen out of the isolette was a huge effort. Like moving a stereo system which still has all its wires and cables attached to the peripherals—some are short, some are long, some are connected here, some there. One wrong move and the whole thing falls to the floor, along with whatever is in the way. We needed two, sometimes three people to accomplish the lift—one to raise Owen's little body, the others to guide the wires and give slack in the lines so that nothing pulled or tugged. There was also a moment of handoff—because the lines were never long enough, I would hover over the rocking chair, about to sit, arms outstretched to receive, ready to ease down immediately as Owen was passed over. I realized later that it wasn't medically necessary for me to wait so long until I first held him—the delay was more about the comfort level of the attending nurse. On day 9, we were assigned a highly competent and unflappable "main" nurse, Lori, who quickly became comfortable with her new charge and expressed surprise when she found out I hadn't held him yet. Lori became Owen's advocate and my ally on the inside. I slept better on those nights when I knew she was on shift.

❖ ❖ ❖ ❖ ❖

Owen weighed 5 pounds when he was born. Normally a good size for a preterm baby but in his case it was mostly fluid. The chest tubes continued to drain excess fluid from his chest cavity and the general stresses of life outside the womb caused some overall shrinkage. He was being fed a low-fat formula through his nasogastric (NG) tube; no specific diagnosis was yet given and apparently his current symptoms could sometimes be associated with an inability to digest fats.

By the second week he had scaled down to about four pounds. Previously kind of plump, he was now scrawny with an unreasonably thin neck. His skin was loose in some places. Abrasions and red marks were left in the spots from which the various sticker pads and IVs had already been moved and removed several times.

He had yet to open his eyes, make typical baby sounds, lift his head or squeeze his hand. But he would cry. He would cry a lot—no wonder, in light of the perpetual insults and indignities of the physical invasions. His eyes would squish tighter, his arms would fling out to the sides, his little body would go rigid and he would holler his lungs out. The odd thing was, he didn't make a sound. The breathing tube that goes through the nostril and down into the lungs also blocks the vocal chords. In those days I would have given anything to hear his wails. When he cried I would try to hold him close to my face so I could feel the warmth of his breath as he let loose. I wanted him to know that someone was paying attention.

It was difficult to get close to him because of the ventilator tubing. There was a connector between the larger hollow blue tube that was attached to the wall and the thinner tubing that entered his nasal passage. In order to keep a good seal, the connector is large—many preemies end up with unevenly stretched nostrils, which they eventually outgrow—and it must be taped to the face to prevent it from dislodging. The connector and tubing are also relatively heavy. The connector and tubing must be held up to maintain slack or it will pull in directions unfortunate and uncomfortable for the patient. IV tubing is different; lines can dangle without support provided they are not at risk of the IV pole rolling over it or someone stepping on it.

To keep things as simple and safe as possible, I was encouraged—if I was going to hold him at all—to settle in for a long while. The slack in the tubing was maintained by taping down all of the lines to the arm of the rocking chair. Because holding Owen meant hunkering down for a few hours, literally taped to the chair, I would prepare the side table ahead of time: glass of water, bedside phone, reading material, a hidden snack.

Most of the time I just sat and rocked, or glided. Until then I hadn't experienced the nifty upholstered sliding armchairs that had become standard in nurseries around the world. I loved the swinging sensation as I pressed back and rebounded forward, all without my feet leaving the floor. Owen and I would glide for hours, relieving the nurse on duty from doing any personal care and leaving her to attend only to the machines, medications and charts.

◆ ◆ ◆ ◆ ◆

Days turned into weeks and weeks turned into months.

I learned to live day to day without knowing when, or even *if*, Owen was coming home. I would arrive at the hospital by 9:00 a.m. and leave every evening between 7:00 p.m. and 9:00 p.m. It became my world. I made friends with other parents, I learned the daily lunch specials. I knew which nurses were rotating on or off, and which doctors would be on duty when.

Although I became immersed in the rhythms of hospital life, I occasionally asked when Owen would be released. Seemed like a different answer every time:

"When he's stronger."

"When he has regular bowel movements."

"When he's more stable."

"When he can breathe on his own."

"When he can tolerate more food."

"When he stops having spells."

Spells: episodes of breath holding (directly observable or not) that would result in a marked drop in oxygen saturation in the blood. This also meant two additional simultaneous events: the persistent beeping of the monitor and Owen's alarmingly sudden blue skin tone. The standard treatment for these episodes was to administer increased oxygen through a mask pressed hard onto the face to maintain a seal, and chest/lung stimulation, continued until his respiration returned to normal and his blood's oxygen saturation elevated to the desired numbers. It was known as "bagging", a reference to the air bag attached to the outside of the mask and manually pumped by the doctor or nurse. As soon as the beeping started, Owen would be dive-bombed by the attending nurses and doctors. It was exhausting for everyone—he would promptly pass out afterwards.

Their resuscitation techniques *seemed* to be effective. He would start out blue and lifeless, and end up pink and breathing. But I had doubts. I wasn't sure that all of this intervention was necessary. I suspected for some time that their efforts were not, in fact, the reason he would "resolve."

It was common practice for parents to exert what little control we felt we had. Rewrapping a diaper, adjusting the blankets, fussing over how the formula cans were arranged. And silencing the alarms. The racket in an intensive care setting is tremendous—challenged in intensity only by the brightness of the lights and the smell of the antibacterial soap and the deep creases in our worried, tired faces.

The alarm is programmed into each machine and set to go off if numbers dip below or elevate above certain preset levels. Similar to a snooze button on a bedside alarm clock, the Silence button would be pressed when the nurse came over to see what was going on. More often than not, it was a sneeze, a stretch, a sleepy movement that would have triggered the alarm, and once the baby settled, all was back to normal. But parents watched this carefully and within a short time knew not only how to silence alarms but also how to turn the oxygen up or down, retape a slipping feeding tube or reposition a wayward monitor lead.

I tested my theory about the ineffectiveness of the nurses' interventions. When the nurse wasn't looking, I turned off the alarm.

❖ ❖ ❖ ❖ ❖

Years later, during a hospitalization for the insertion of Owen's permanent feeding tube, I'd had quite enough of the temporary feeding tube that had been inserted down through his nose. (The nasogastric (NG) tube is very thin; it travels up one nostril, down the back of the throat and ends in the stomach.) I asked if we could please remove it as he didn't need it anymore and it was irritating his skin and throat. He had been receiving most of his feeds through the new g-tube and by all accounts the procedure had been successful.

"No, not yet," the nurse said, "the doctor didn't say it could come out. We can ask when he comes back later."

My mind immediately switched to a different mode. Scheming, plotting.

"What if it becomes dislodged," I asked. "What if his flailing hand catches it and he pulls it out? What then?"

"Oh, I doubt we'll reinsert it in that case," she said. She gathered up the empty food cans and used tubing, and left.

I stayed seated on the bed and counted to ten to be sure. Then I got up and slowly closed the door, looking at Owen meaningfully. He grinned. I carefully removed the pink tape from his face, holding on to the thin tube so that it wouldn't irritate his throat or stomach. Then slowly and steadily, I eased the NG-tube out completely. He coughed a bit, sputtered, then laughed his most hearty laugh.

Some hours later, the shift changed and the new nurse came in to discharge us. She didn't even notice.

❖ ❖ ❖ ❖ ❖

I had developed confidence over time, starting with those many weeks in Intensive Care with Owen. I knew the spells were holding him back from being discharged, and at this rate we would be there forever. I decided it was time to see if we could stop the assaults and let him rebound from the spells naturally, if that was in fact what would happen. I tested my theory by turning the alarm off completely and watching him closely.

Sure enough, within minutes, he had another spell. Without warning he grew, at first imperceptibly and then noticeably, limp as his pallor changed from pale pink to slightly grey-tinged to a kind of weird baby blue. I gently repositioned him upright, watching his face carefully, ready to yell for a nurse if this all went awry.

After approximately the same amount of time it would have taken for the nurse and respiratory therapist to come running over and blast more oxygen in his face—maybe ten seconds—Owen gasped lightly, then inhaled deeply. He coughed, stretched, and began to pink up again. Slightly dazed but no worse for wear. Certainly less exhausted than if he'd been resuscitated.

It was an ongoing tension between the nurses and me—I would hide his spells from them, sometimes successfully sometimes not. If I wasn't there they would, of course, do what they were trained to do. It would not have done any good to point this out to the nurses, as they can't override their instructions for treatment. Instead, I asked for a case meeting, organized by Lori, so we could review Owen's treatment plan.

Eventually, the order was written: "No more bagging. Baby will resolve on his own." It was my first lesson in advocacy.

❖ ❖ ❖ ❖ ❖

Owen was finally discharged in mid-November, three months after he was born, one month after his due date.

# Five

> Owen has no independent mobility of any sort. His hands are usually closed, and he demonstrates dystonic posturing when he gets excited. His parents use a variety of "environmental engineering" techniques to make toys and objects available to him, given his lack of independent motor control.
>
> **Pediatric Developmental Clinic, August 20, 2000**

For a while in the late 90s the Gap was running Baby Gap ads with nothing but big baby faces. I got my hands on all I could find. I even bought magazines solely for those ads. They were perfect teaching aids. "Eyes!" "Baby!" "Happy!" Apparently babies like looking at pictures of other babies, so these photos were ideal. Some of the ads were cut out and pasted into scrapbooks. The best ones, ones in which faces were perfectly round and squishy, I reserved for a particular purpose.

I made a small box out of cardboard and pasted a baby ad to each side. I fastened decorative bows, sparkles and ribbons. I attached a rubber band chain to the top and dangled it from a floor-standing baby activity centre. I positioned Owen under it so he could see the amusing faces and bat at the box. The structure was used through many months of therapy and play, and withstood many different dangling appendages of which the homemade Baby Gap box was one. I often changed it seasonally. For several weeks I replaced the hanging box with draped, shiny bead necklaces and Christmas bead strands—he would look up at the glistening balls and fidget with his fingers until he'd scrunched the necklaces so tight in his sweaty fist the painted coating would rub off. Sometimes he would get tangled and I would have to free him. I rigged up suspended stuffed animals, dolls and rubber ducks.

Owen didn't play with regular toys, which was fine with me! This cut down on the clutter, and challenged me as I tried to figure out what would amuse him.

"Here, try this..."

Owen's occupational therapist at the time, Sandra, approved of my makeshift contraptions. We would experiment with textures, tastes, sensations. If Owen couldn't be out in the world like a regular kid, we would bring the world to him.

On one occasion Sandra handed me a stalk of celery. I looked at the small green stick. Celery? Was she nuts? Owen had razor sharp teeth but couldn't yet chew. Wouldn't he chomp the end off and choke on it?

She handed me a square of cotton mesh cheesecloth.

"Wrap the end of the celery in it. Some kids like the crunch and the mesh will stop the piece from going down his throat." Brilliant! Sandra was full of creative ideas.

The trial flopped—one of Owen's jagged teeth snagged the mesh bag and it took us a few minutes to untangle the mess from his mouth. One of us had to pry open his jaw while the other diligently picked out the bits of thread.

But it got my wheels turning: "Where can I get more ideas?"

She happened to have some handouts she'd been carrying for another client. Tips for making scented playdough, activities involving dried beans and bare feet, more hints for practising chewing. She loaded me up with paper, and I started a binder for future visits.

"There's also this... You might want to take a look." She looked pleased. It was a catalogue of specialty equipment for disabled kids.

I didn't even open it. "I don't think there's anything in there—but thanks anyway." If there was a change of tone in my voice, she didn't hear it, or didn't acknowledge it.

"Sure there is . . ." She flipped to an interior page. "What about something like this . . . ?"

She pointed to a blue and red rubbery-looking moulded seat with a carved out back and sectional pieces attached with industrial-strength Velcro.

"Like this one. It's a custom floor seat. He can sit up a bit, see the world, reach to midline more easily."

Oh, come on, I thought. Owen is just a bit behind. These kids have real problems. He's not like that.

"I suppose. I could see how for some of those kids it might be useful."

I held the catalogue casually, daring myself to look further to show her and myself that I wasn't afraid of anything, that I was a progressive mom, that I could look at a catalogue and be open-minded and look at the nice disabled kids who—by the way—were nothing like Owen. A panic rose up: Is this the future she saw for him?

Tricycles, special cups, seating systems . . . Wait, what's that? An awkwardly tall kid, maybe 12 years old, strapped into a standing frame. The base was royal blue; the fabric padding and straps were brightly coloured in primary tones. It looked like a Hannibal-Lecter-style imprisoning body cage, for kids. (When a few years later we acquired that standing frame, the first of many, not a few jokes were cracked about Owen having the scariest Halloween costume. But that was still years away. At this moment, Owen was unique, not disabled.)

The boy was strapped in firmly and standing upright, standing against the back of the frame as though he were standing against a wall. A supporting bracket was positioned over his knees to prevent them from buckling. Short side panels prevented the hips and ribs from jutting to one side or another and wide straps were positioned at hip and chest level. A clear plastic tray was mounted in front.

The boy in the picture was laughing. Inside, I was dying. I couldn't help myself: "Wow, that must be tough."

"What must be tough?" She peered over at the picture.

"Having a big kid and needing something for him to even just stand up." What I meant was, having a big kid like *that*. The whole thing was an assault on my eyes. Appalling. Sad.

Sandra sensed the change in my tone. She looked at the picture, then chose her words carefully. "Well . . . It's maybe hard at first but if it gives the child more function and opportunities to socialize, the parents are usually glad they have it."

I shrugged. "I suppose."

I handed the catalogue to Sandra; she closed it and put it back in her bag.

# Six

Playgrounds often saddened me. What do I do with Owen? Why are we here anyway? He can't sit in those swings—not even in the bucket-style ones with space for legs to dangle. I wedged him into one once and, when I couldn't get him out, I had to ask a playground dad for help. Later that day, when I changed him, I saw deep pressure grooves on the insides of his legs.

He couldn't sit in the sand, neither could he slide. I could take him down the slide with me but it was uncomfortable on my ass, wider now because I was pregnant with Angus. If it was a twisty slide I would have to pull myself down in stages, with my heels. I was only good for going down once or twice.

So we busied ourselves by watching, positioning ourselves near other children running around, somewhere out of direct sunlight, close to other moms in the futile hope of striking up a conversation.

Michael and I occasionally took Justin to a playground we called Pirate Ship Park. Located in an east end neighbourhood, it had a climbing structure built to look like a sunken pirate ship sticking out of the ground. When Owen and I were getting out a bit, doing mom and kid things, that's where I would occasionally take him.

Not that we'd been in hiding, but we didn't have anywhere to go. Our lives were consumed with home appointments and hospital visits. I had tried some community playgroups and drop-in centres but they were unsuitable—they were attended mostly by nannies with their charges, and there were never any kids there like mine. I felt out of place.

I found Toronto moms in my area a tough crowd to penetrate. They were either running by with jogging strollers or having lattes with their sisters-in-law, marching down sidewalks two abreast, occupying coffee shops. I was outwardly critical but inwardly jealous. So I usually sat and watched them, working hard to look occupied but none the less approachable—rather than looking lonely.

On one occasion, a neighbour approached me about joining a mom's stroller group. Brisk walks through the park, stop by the drop-in centre, grab a coffee at Starbucks with new moms, all glowing and chatty.

I was happy she'd asked. "Sure! Let me know when."

Then, slowly, a look of embarrassed concern came over her face—eyebrows suddenly furrow, chin crunches, overall face quickly develops an I-just-remembered-something look.

"A-a-c-tually . . . one of the girls is a little nervous."

I should have walked away then. Who says "girls" anymore?

"Let me check if she's okay with you coming. She gets kind of emotional. Might have a hard time with Owen there."

Come again? I felt the impulse to punch her, but I didn't. I recoiled into myself, told myself that not everyone is as together as I am and that I should be tolerant.

"Ok. Just let me know."

I avoided her after that, dodging inside when she went for a walk. She eventually moved, and I didn't hear from her again.

So it was not with a mom's group that Owen and I made our way to Pirate Ship Park on a windy summer day. I yanked Owen's stroller backwards through the sand and headed toward the play structures. As we sat on a bench I scanned the playground. My gaze rested on the pirate ship. Maybe Owen would enjoy standing on the deck, feeling the change in elevation, putting one tight fist against the helm and feeling it turn. No, too windy. And how would I manage it? I'd carry him because I didn't want to put him back in the stroller only to take him out again, but would have to drag the stroller with me because I wouldn't want to leave it unattended. We'd go up top for no more than 20 seconds, and then what? It probably wasn't worth it.

Wait! There was more to the ship under the deck! He'll love that! We can watch the kids overhead. We'll just relocate. Looks like there are benches underneath.

I dragged the stroller back through the sand. I held him cradled close to my chest while I hunched protectively, ducking under. We fumbled and lurched our way towards the bench over on the far side of the play structure. I sat down hard on the little seat.

Owen loved sand. He couldn't sit but if I wedged him between my knees and held him firmly by the armpits, he could sort of stand. Socks off! Toes squishing in the sand, some smooth rocks inserted into tight fists. A sensory activity.

Thirty seconds go by. I felt eyes on me. I was becoming familiar with feeling watched.

I looked up and met the eyes of a very young boy, sitting across from me on the opposite bench. I didn't know he was there. Staring, mouth agape. Didn't look away when I looked up. He looked at Owen, then looked at me, then again at Owen. I turned my mouth in a half smile then went back to my business.

Now maybe a minute had gone by. Still, staring and gaping. Stop it, kid!

"Hi there." I smiled bigger. But fake.

. . . Nothing. No change in his demeanour. In my head: stop staring. Get lost, brat. Go find your parents. Yes, he's weird and so are you.

"Do you have any questions you'd like to ask?" It was my standard question to small children. In my mind, preparing answers for:

"Why is he like that?"

"What's wrong with him?"

"Is that a boy or a girl?"

"Can't he talk?"

The boy didn't miss a beat. "Does he ever blink?"

I laughed. Jolted out of my irritation.

I might as well give him something to tell his friends. "No," I said. "No, he doesn't. "

"Cool."

## Seven

My private world with my son was magical. I loved him beyond measure. I loved our little family and our wacky ways. It hadn't yet occurred to me that my life was harder than most, that the challenges of parenting Owen were not typical. I just thought the world wasn't ready for him yet. Friends would look upon us warily, make suggestions:

"Maybe you need some help?"

I would say, "Oh, no, we're fine! Besides, I don't want my child raised by a nanny! This is how it's done all over the world!"

Of course I was speaking from the place where babies are not on ventilators or having surgeries or being perpetually sleepless or struggling to breathe or failing to develop. It was the place I thought I was in, or where I wanted to be—not the place in the world I actually was. I was speaking the language of the privileged urban mother who not only could afford a nanny but could afford to *not* have a nanny.

My tolerance for this new life was ratcheting up—I had lost perspective on what normal was. Or rather, I thought I was indeed having a typical parenting experience. After all, aren't all babies sometimes fussy? Don't all babies stay up at night?

❖ ❖ ❖ ❖ ❖

The persistent lack of sleep was starting to take a toll. At night, Michael and I worked shifts to relieve each other of Owen when it was clear that a breaking point was moments away. Something about Owen's sense of space and balance required that he be rocked, swayed and jiggled in order to fall asleep. And for many months, he would only stay asleep if the motion was continuous. I learned to doze propped in the corner of the sofa, Owen nestled in the crook of one arm, which was in turn propped on a firm pillow for support. My body knew the drill, establishing a compromise between my arm and my brain. As though to give my brain a chance to rest, my arm would go on auto-pilot, jiggling at first then slowing to rhythmic muscle contractions to give Owen just enough movement that he wouldn't wake.

Sometimes my mind would swim and my mood would go dark. I wasn't conscious of particular thoughts—I didn't, for instance, have violent fantasies, as do some overtired new mothers—but there were other warning signs that I was reaching my limit. The back of my neck would become uncomfortably warm, the cuddly loving feelings would begin to dissipate, my hold on his little body would become a little more rigid than before. I would get up noisily, sigh heavily, move around the house to induce Michael to wake up and feel sorry for me. But he had learned to sleep through my suffering as I had learned to sleep through his, knowing it would be his turn "on duty" soon enough.

Occasionally, frustration would turn to hostility. I would plunk Owen down on the bed beside Michael knowing that his fidgeting and cries would eventually wake him. "I'm done. You take him." Then I would leave to go downstairs to sleep in the living room, closing the door solidly behind me.

❖ ❖ ❖ ❖ ❖

Owen was almost a year old when I agreed to our first government agency supplied respite worker and applied for individual funding to hire additional help.

Mostly, I used the respite time to catch up on sleep.

# Eight

Unaided results have consistently been obtained at levels that corroborate his initial ABR suggesting severe to profound loss.

In regards to your queries about what is audible to Owen, and the quality of the auditory signal he receives, I think we can be sure that even with the hearing aids, many speech sounds are likely to be inaudible to him. Typically for his configuration of hearing loss, some of the lower frequency sounds (some of the vowels and consonants such as g, b) are audible to some extent, but high frequency information is lost (sounds like, s, sh, ch, t, p, f, th, etc) This can result in awareness that there is some input, but being unable to extract enough information for the input to be intelligible. People with sensorineural loss also have a significant amount of distortion in the auditory system so that even when a sound is amplified and audible to some degree, it may be quite distorted or unclear.

**Department of Communication Disorders, Audiology, November 30, 2004**

"It's really quite profound."

Owen's level of hearing loss was determined to be in the severe-to-profound range of the audiology chart. The audiologist confirmed this for us after Owen's hearing test, conducted at around the age of 3 months. We suspected as much already—his auditory tests in the neonatal intensive care unit had come back flat (no response), and we noticed that he didn't respond to sound.

But with a child in Owen's condition, things can develop at an unpredictable pace, so we'd left room for the idea that we might eventually find out he could, after all, hear.

It wasn't to be. When I first heard the news of Owen's profound hearing loss, I wasn't upset. Although Owen's deafness would prove to be the biggest obstacle to his meaningful participation in anything social—greater than his inability to walk, sit, stand, crawl or eat independently—it felt, at that moment, like a small problem.

Oh well, I thought. At least he can see!

The doctor was apologetic. "I'm so sorry," she said. "I imagine this is upsetting. I'm sure it's not what you wanted to hear." She sorted through some papers and produced a brochure, a follow-up appointment card to the hospital's HEAR clinic, and the phone number for another mom whose child had also been diagnosed with profound hearing loss a couple of years earlier.

My good mood declined. I sighed. I resigned myself to investigating the doctor's recommendations.

❖ ❖ ❖ ❖ ❖

"Mommy! I can hear the crickets!"

A fairy tale was drifting through the telephone: a young boy diagnosed with profound loss had recovered from cochlear implant surgery, received ongoing auditory-verbal therapy. The intervention worked and a family initially devastated upon learning of the boy's deafness turns jubilant. The boy's mom finishes recounting the story that ended with the chirping crickets and starts to cry.

" 'Mommy! I can hear the crickets!' We had worked so hard to finally hear those words!"

Fair enough. Who wouldn't want their child to hear crickets? What parent wouldn't do whatever it takes for their child to hear such sweet sounds? To hear the crickets—a metaphor for living a normal, fulfilled life.

"Oh sure, yes, it would be great if Owen could hear crickets too. Thank you for sharing your story. Certainly, I will let you know how things go . . ."

I hung up the phone. I hadn't found Owen's hearing loss depressing until now.

❖ ❖ ❖ ❖ ❖

The diagnosis was made at The Hospital for Sick Children (Sick Kids) in Toronto. Its HEAR program—Hearing Evaluation and Rehabilitation—was a leader in treating children with hearing loss.

Profound hearing loss cannot really be treated or fixed. Hearing aids or speech therapy alone would not have helped. Instead, for children with Owen's type of hearing loss, parents can opt for the cochlear implant—a device implanted in the skull with a corresponding receiver that clips into the hair, receiving and transmitting sounds to the implant conveying information that the brain would not otherwise receive and process. The device is implanted on the side with the lesser hearing ability, destroying any residual hearing that might have been there before the surgery.

The implant itself is just the start—then follow years of speech and language therapy to help the child identify, interpret and locate the sounds being transmitted.

❖ ❖ ❖ ❖ ❖

I did not ask for the implant. I didn't even know about it. But not long after we received the diagnosis, I got a call from the hospital for an appointment.

"You're on the implant list!" The receptionist said it so enthusiastically that I felt compelled to confirm the appointment.

❖ ❖ ❖ ❖ ❖

The hospital lined up a team of specialists to meet with us, including a social worker to answer our questions and direct us to any further resources if required.

The social worker was a nice woman. We chatted about success rates, required follow-on therapies, follow-up appointments, time commitments. I listened politely, but really only wanted to know if there were any alternatives to the implant procedure. Surely there are deaf people out there who lead productive lives without such extreme intervention.

"Oh, well, sure," she said. "If you're into signing and stuff like that."

❖ ❖ ❖ ❖ ❖

Success stories were very important to the program. My impression was that their funding depended on it. We attended an "information session" later that week, presided over by the head of the program. We learned little about the actual procedure but sat through a PowerPoint presentation, complete with numbers and graphs. The message was repeated several times: we need more successful candidates to fulfill our funding requirements.

How, exactly, was this an *information* session? More importantly, how was this meeting appropriate for us, or any other parent? Maybe I had misunderstood what the session was for.

This wasn't the first time I felt a greater marketing engine at work.

As it happens, on the day of our first appointment with the HEAR clinic, the hospital was celebrating its 100th cochlear implant procedure. We were invited down to the lobby after our appointment to appreciate the success of the program. We were treated to the preening of the program doctors, the fawning of the grateful parents, the glare of the media cameras, pieces of free cake.

An early recipient of the implant was there, giving interviews — a preteen girl who could now, thanks to the implant, talk on the phone, hear whispers, and almost—*almost*—talk like she could hear.

The procedure is now commonplace and an accepted "remedy" for deafness that the vast majority of hearing parents choose for their deaf children. But it was new to me, and I thought it was creepy. I wasn't yet familiar with why signing deaf people felt so threatened by it, or why it was likened to ethnic cleansing, or why it was such a divisive topic between the deaf and hearing communities, but I had a sense that something was *off*. Something was missing. My instinct was to reject the implant procedure. And besides, I was so grateful Owen was alive it didn't occur to me to be upset that he was deaf.

❖ ❖ ❖ ❖ ❖

I developed a good working relationship with Owen's audiologist. I picked her brain every time we saw her, and wondered about the implant, about hearing aids, about speech therapy, about sign language. She could sense my implicit reluctance to cut open a perfectly good head.

One day, not long after the initial HEAR program appointments, she passed me a business card like it was an illicit substance. She happened to give it to me when no one was around. Or did she wait for the right moment?

"Maybe you'd like another perspective? Talk to the director. She can help answer your questions."

The card was for an organization called Silent Voice, a deaf advocacy and literacy organization that recognizes the cultural uniqueness of people who use sign language to communicate. I phoned as soon as I returned home from the appointment.

The director asked me, "Have you ever met a deaf person?" What a good question. The hospital never asked me that.

"No."

"Would you like to?" The director knew a family who would be happy to meet me. All family members were deaf with profound loss, except a son, whose hearing loss was moderate The mother and son came to our house for a conversation, and it was a revelation. I was struck by the ease with which we all communicated. How the mom could float between ASL and speech without missing a beat, how well adjusted the son was.

He told us, "Don't do it. Accept him for who he is."

I thought, finally a way out! I could learn to sign instead of trying to make Owen learn to hear.

❖ ❖ ❖ ❖ ❖

Yes, signing is beautiful. It's also really hard to get right. Deaf people know this. Many are tolerant of a poor signer. Some are not. Hearing people, by comparison are stiff, inexpressive, unvaried. We rely on words to describe and our bodies often don't move as we talk. There is nothing more boring to a deaf person than standing in the midst of a group of talking people.

ASL (American Sign Language) requires a deep physicality and comfort with one's own body. Facial expression, body position, use of hands as "classifiers" (hand-shape substitutes for actual people or people in the context of the story, like using your fingers to show walking to the store . . .)—these are real and important parts of the language and sentence syntax. People unfamiliar with ASL might think of this as acting or miming, or a way of emoting. But the language is much more complex and nuanced than that.

We arranged an ASL tutor through Silent Voice. It took me years to become fluent; books, courses and tutoring did not fully prepare me for the intensity of real interaction and engagement. I didn't develop good conversational skills until I started to hire deaf support workers for Owen. But as a new student I was enthusiastic and receptive, eager to learn the language and understand more about deafness and the deaf community. The more I learned, the more I knew we were headed in the right direction.

Not long after that first meeting with the Deaf family, I wrote a letter to the HEAR clinic and told them to take Owen's name off the cochlear implant list.

# Nine

> Our primary communication focus and goal for Owen at school was to encourage him to establish a consistent mode of communication to enable him to make choices and requests on a regular basis. In consultation with you and [a therapist], we determined that we would encourage Owen to communicate using eye gaze. Owen used his eye gaze to engage adults and children and to share his focus of attention for toys and objects that he liked . . . However, at school we felt Owen did not make consistent choices. His inability to do so was often due to his tone and discomfort in his chair.
>
> Owen always sat on his volunteer's lap and across from the teacher at music and story time. He thoroughly enjoyed the physical movement during the songs. He was aware of the children next to him sleeping like little bunnies and he smiled when we hopped around him. Owen opened his eyes wide with anticipation and excitement when the monkey snapped out of the tree.
>
> **Preschool Report, June 15, 2001**

Sending Owen off to nursery school was nerve-wracking. He was just 2 years old, riding a bus with other disabled kids in a mini-van taxi driven by someone with no training in childcare or in managing children with special needs. I would buckle him into his seat in the morning and then eagerly await his exhausted, sweaty return 3 hours later. On most days, my only sense of daily life at school came through the Communication Book.

I would write: "Owen had a small breakfast so he might be hungry when he arrives." Or, "Owen had a good night's sleep!" In return, I would read: "Owen had a lot of fun today! He made a new friend." "Owen was a good helper at snacktime." "Owen slept through music but really liked gym."

Centennial Infant and Child Centre was a sweet place in midtown

Toronto, complete with rubbery floor mats, amusing decorations and dedicated, knowledgeable staff. Every day, a homemade bright yellow book with a laminated cover would appear in his backpack—loopy handwriting recounting the day's events and small moments. I ate it up! I would devour every word, every smiley face, every exclamation mark. I wanted to be part of his day, hear about his adventures. He couldn't tell me himself, so I relied on the book. I was also looking for an indication that Owen was improving and developing. I searched for signs of intelligence, ability, potential.

I loved that he was having these experiences, shared with such enthusiasm in the little book. I imagined the scene: like a pen pal writing a thoughtful note to a far-away friend in Japan, Owen's helper would reflect on the day, pick only the very best moments to share because there were so many . . . laugh to herself as she recalled an amusing moment.

❖ ❖ ❖ ❖ ❖

I came to school early one day to pick up Owen for an appointment at the hospital, so there was no need for him to take the bus home. We weren't in a rush so I decided to wait off to the side until the teacher had dismissed the class.

Volunteers and staff scrambled around retrieving socks, diapers, bags. I sat patiently and looked around. Pleasant chaos, friendly chatter, tired children. The facility was small and space was at a premium, but somehow, they managed to keep the space playful and inviting.

As I waited, I observed the teacher sitting on one of the mats—the teacher on whose every scribbled, enthusiastic word I hung my day's happiness. She was surrounded by the tumbled remains of a stack of at least fifteen books, whipping off sentence after happy sentence and looking a little frazzled.

"Wait! Don't let the buses go yet! I'm almost done!" She didn't look up as she tossed a little yellow book into the finished pile then picked up the next one and started scribbling.

How could she write so fast? I wondered: did she write the same thing in every book? Or did she do what I always suspected grade school teachers do: rotate sentences randomly?

Earlier that month, the book came back with "Owen especially loved the hokey-pokey!" We were so touched after reading that, Michael made it his private joke with Owen, one of their sweet father-son connections—Michael would gather him into his lap and perform an adapted version of the hokey-pokey song and dance. Michael would look at me with a twinkle in his eye, his face full of emotion, and say, "Owen loves the hokey-pokey."

Did other children's dads also hang on these words? Did all of the students "love the hokey-pokey"? Was the hokey-pokey now the assumed favourite of Centennial nursery students everywhere?

At that moment, when I saw the fast scribbling and hurried wrap-up to the day, I understood that the comments in the book aren't always to be taken literally. They suggest a flavour to the day by providing a sense of things that happened at one point or another, a feeling of activity and enjoyment and taking care. It was a busy place with lots to do—the books couldn't possibly capture everything.

I understood that and yet something shifted in me. I didn't stop reading the communication books or looking for great moments in Owen's day, but I would occasionally need to suppress a new, unfamiliar feeling. A welling pessimism and suspicion and a tendency to wonder if it's all pretence.

Maybe it was. And maybe we needed the gentle fabrications and the wishful thinking and the projected fantasy to keep the wheels greased and the engine running and everyone feeling useful.

# Ten

I am writing to you regarding Owen, who is a 4-year old boy with a documented diagnosis of spastic quadriplegia cerebral palsy. Owen is dependent in all of his activities of daily living including dressing, bathing, grooming, feeding, toileting and transfers. He is using a manual wheelchair and is dependent on his parents to transfer him in and out of his wheelchair, to transfer him in and out of his stander, and to transfer him on and off surfaces such as the floor, bed, and in and out of the bathtub. As well, parents are lifting him in and out of the car. Presently, the parents are also lifting the manual wheelchair in and out of the car for transport.

**Prescription letter for wheelchair van funding,
May 12, 2003**

"Whatever you do, don't move north of Steeles."

Our house had become too small and it was time to make a decision. Owen had recently acquired his first piece of large equipment—a standing frame. A huge apparatus with an H-shaped base designed to support the swivelling standing frame on the top. Tilted back, we could place Owen on it flat in order to strap him in, legs straightened, hips aligned, spine in order. Attach the knee-block so he wouldn't buckle with weight bearing. Head support so he wouldn't slump. Lock the wheels and slowly tip the frame upright until he was standing, more or less.

The frame itself was very heavy—easily eighty pounds. Small plastic castors ensured poor mobility and a bumpy ride for Owen. It was garishly ugly with a royal blue coating on the metal frame and a loud childish print on the straps. (It was identical to the one I had seen in the catalogue, less than two years before.) The footprint of the base was about 5 feet by 4 feet so the whole thing wouldn't tip over when Owen was in it.

We already owned a custom "seating system" which could tilt and recline and which had a hydraulic base that could elevate and lower him. It also had an outdoor base into which we could insert the seat itself, so it transformed into a stroller. This was relatively small, taking up the same space as a large highchair.

The stander was different. It may not have been the exact thing that initiated our need to move, but looking back it's as good a thing as any other to pin it on. The equipment, the larger wheelchair we knew he would eventually need, and general accessibility in and out of the house all played a part. We knew we had to move.

"The Toronto District School Board has signing programs for deaf kids. York Region doesn't. Everything is oral up there. Just stay south of Steeles."

No problem! I didn't even know where Steeles *was*. Somewhere out in the suburbs. We were downtowners, living in a Victorian semi in Leslieville. My life was downtown. Michael's office was located in the north end of the city but he didn't mind—he commuted against traffic and mostly worked from home. And the school programs didn't matter—I was intending to homeschool anyway.

We looked first in our adjacent neighbourhoods, visiting inaccessible house after inaccessible house, imagining ramps, elevators, lifts. Every house was wrong or a hopeless cause—our radius of tolerance widened to include areas north of Bloor, then north of St. Clair (heading dangerously into North Toronto, which we couldn't afford), leafy Leaside and retro Parkside Hills to the east. For reasons I don't quite remember, crossing Yonge to the west was not even an option. We also spent an inordinate amount of time investigating an infill new-house project in a trashy neighbourhood in East York. The builder was unhelpful and dragged his heels in sorting out the need for an elevator.

We weren't yet despairing, but concern was setting in. We had already sold our current house and were working on a deadline.

"I found the perfect house!"

Michael's voice was echo-y. He was in the basement of an undecorated model home, which hadn't yet sold. A large bungalow-style house, 2,300 square feet on one floor.

"Where is it?"

"You have to see how huge this basement is! The living spaces are so open! There's a park and playground right across the street!"

It sounded fantastic.

"Where is it?"

"A bit north. You have to see it."

◆ ◆ ◆ ◆ ◆

The Town of Markham. A small city in the Region of York, whose southern border touches the City of Toronto at Steeles Avenue. Driving north on Markham Road from the 401 you see stretches of industrial park, a Leon's furniture outlet, several strip malls with diners, Asian grocers and discount stores. At Steeles itself stands a "Welcome to the Town of Markham" sign over a water fountain which occasionally overflows with soap bubbles that spill onto the street, evidence of some bored teenagers' high jinks.

Further on, Asian restaurants, knock-off fast food restaurants and coffee chains (Coffee Lime?). Just beyond that stretch, big box stores, a Costco and a Food Basics. Turn right onto 14th Avenue, make your way to Legacy.

The sky was bleak and grey. No fluffy snow this time of year, no signs of spring. Just cold and bare.

I pulled up to the house, noticing the playground and parkland across the street. I pushed open the front door—unlocked as Michael reported—and looked around. I slowly walked around, imagining our family in this space. The house wasn't quite finished yet, but Michael was right. It was perfect for us. Damn.

❖ ❖ ❖ ❖ ❖

I gave myself pep talks. We'll do it for Owen. For Angus. We need more space and we drive everywhere anyway. And I'm not working. It's only Michael's job location that matters and this is way closer for him. I still plan to homeschool the boys so whatever the therapist said about school programming doesn't matter.

Friends said: "I grew up in the suburbs! It's not so bad!"

Our real-estate agent had become a friend. "It's a great house, " he joked. "I'll never come visit you, but it's a great house!"

❖ ❖ ❖ ❖ ❖

Markham was good to us. I found services, help for Owen, friendly moms in the park. Toronto fell away—it simply became the place where Sick Kids and Bloorview were, where Michael worked, where I used to live before I moved north. We built a deck, landscaped the front yard, painted the back wall of the living room a Ralph Lauren red.

I had thought Markham would be too homogenous. When I discovered the multicultural mix of the neighbourhood, I was happy to note that I had been wrong after all. Neighbours on one side were originally from China, on the other, from Pakistan. Waves of technology professionals from distant lands had settled in our little neck of the woods—Silicon Valley North, the Town of Markham called itself. Legacy was a more ethnically diverse and wealthier neighbourhood than I had imagined, or ever lived in before.

But unfortunately, the suburban lifestyle wiped out any chance of mingling or getting to know anyone else—black, brown, yellow or otherwise. Everyone, including us, had a remote control for the garage door. Drive out, drive in. When the door descended behind the rear end of the minivan, the house was essentially closed for the night. The homes in our neighbourhood didn't have street-facing living rooms. They had "great rooms" off the kitchen, which usually faced the backyard. Even in the early evening, it was hard to tell if anyone was home. From the street, everything looked shut down.

The playground was largely empty except immediately after school dismissal. On weekends, our neighbourhood was a ghost town. Everyone was either inside, or away.

Good thing our house was big, with bright, open and airy spaces. Our basement was full-size—the full footprint of the house. Although the downstairs walls, ceiling and floor were unfinished, we fashioned a huge playroom, yoga studio, guest bedroom, with carpets on the concrete floor and curtains acting as dividers.

I loved that house. And right up to the day we agreed I should move out, I wished it stood anywhere other than where it was.

# Eleven

In general Jennifer identified her goals at this time to include participation, enjoyment, socialization, interaction with peers, adjustment to other students and different environments. Jennifer hopes that his time in the Kindergarten will also provide a valuable perspective for the other students and a respect for individual differences.

Her goals for Owen's time at Senior Kindergarten do not focus on academics or skill-building—she plans to continue home-schooling and developing Owen's skills at home where it is quiet and less disruptive. Thus, exact adaptations of the academic programme are not always necessary: the process, active participation and social interaction with peers and making things meaningful at Owen's level are Jennifer's overall goals.

**Communication and Writing Aids Service, Client Service Plan, November 27, 2003**

Long before moving to Markham I had decided that I would eventually homeschool both children, and Michael was supportive. I had thought of Owen's special needs preschool as more like babysitting, and I wasn't interested in regular public school for either of the boys. But several months after the move I had grown weary. The boys' needs were very different and I couldn't keep up. When Angus was four, he started attending a nursery program at a Waldorf school. I decided Owen should go to school too. I was looking forward to a break from both boys simultaneously.

Boxwood Public School, where Owen was to attend kindergarten in 2003, was in the next neighbourhood over. The school is part of the York Region District School Board, which does not officially identify children as having disabilities until they are in the first grade. Owen would be in a regular kindergarten class and was, as far as I could tell, the only one with visible disabilities. His classmates would be kids from the neighbourhood—kids we usually saw in the playground and on the street—and the children of my own adult friends.

The school had never before dealt with someone like Owen. The assigned classroom assistant, although in place to support the whole class, would essentially become his personal support worker—diapering, facilitating, transitioning. Everyone was eager and supportive, but scared stiff.

That is, everyone was scared stiff except the children. They embraced him as one of their own. Sometimes curious, sometimes indifferent, always accepting his presence and participation as a given.

The classroom was under-equipped to handle a child like Owen so I brought in as much equipment from home as I could. I purchased an additional stander to leave in the classroom. A gym mat served as an on-the-floor change table in the class bathroom until the assistant reasonably complained that the floor was sticky and smelled like pee and was not a dignified place to change Owen, after which the mat was moved to another room. He had a folding lawn chair for circle time, a head support and a box of adapted toys and switches, all left at the school.

For the first two weeks I brought Owen in and picked him up myself. (Once everyone was familiar with the routine, he rode the accessible school bus to and from school.) At first, the assistant looked completely overwhelmed—red-cheeked, frizzy-haired, perpetually frazzled. But within a month she was an old pro; competent, affectionate, keen. She, too, would write in a communication book. But with only one child to write about, her remarks were typically candid and thorough.

One day, an envelope came home in Owen's backpack, Owen's name printed in marker on the front, the flap of the envelope unsealed but tucked in. I pulled out a child's invitation card.

"*Owen* is invited to a *birthday party* for *Miller!*"

For real? Was it a pity invite? I had to know. I cornered the mom in the playground.

"*So*, we got the invite from Miller . . ."

"Oh good! Should be a fun time."

"*So*, I guess the whole class was invited . . . ?"

"No. Just a few kids. Miller wrote a list."

Miller wrote a list. And Owen's name was on it! Was this voluntary? Using all the tools in my mental and verbal arsenal, I danced around the conversation until I was sure.

"Yes, he was very clear about whom he wanted to invite. When he read me the list Owen's name was right in the middle."

Right in the middle! That clinched it. Not at the top where it obviously would not be a real invite, and not at the bottom where I would assume he was an afterthought. Owen's first real birthday party invitation! I relished that feeling for days.

# Twelve

The following recommendations were discussed with OT's mother and provided in writing at the time of the assessment.
1. Thicken all liquids to a thin puree consistency or thicker.
2. Nectar consistency liquids and thin liquids are NOT SAFE.
3. Positioning: OT MUST be positioned in his seating system with hips flexed to 90 degrees, sitting upright, with his <u>head in neutral</u>. OT is at risk of aspiration/penetration when his neck is extended.
4. After feeds, keep OT in an upright position for about an hour.
5. Pace: 30 seconds between spoons
6. Amount: 1/4 - 1/2 teaspoon amounts
7. Use an empty spoon to stimulate a swallow in between every 2nd spoon of food.
8. Thicken feeds to a medium puree or thick puree when OT is ill or fatigued.
9. Continue with tooth-brushing twice daily.

**Videofluoroscopic Swallow Study Report,
October 28, 2002**

When Owen was born and still in intensive care, he was first fed through a temporary feeding tube, then through a bottle. Because of his precarious health and the doctors' uncertainty about his ability to digest proteins Owen was, for his first few weeks, given a low-fat formula. But during the same period, I was pumping and saving breast milk in the hopes that he would be able to consume it. Eventually, he was given my breast milk by bottle, doled out in sequence—first the fatty colostrum then the more usual-looking, slightly watery milk.

Over the many weeks of pumping, we accumulated a considerable stock of milk. I used hospital urine bottles to keep the frozen milk, producing up to 10 full bottles a day. We bought a small freezer to hold it all. I understand now that I didn't really need to pump that much—I could have reduced the milk by pumping less frequently, then ramped up production to be ready for Owen's homecoming. That would certainly have been less taxing—I had been waking in the night to pump when Owen wasn't yet home from the hospital.

I was eventually able to breastfeed Owen—a lovely but often physically gruelling experience. Owen had high tone and reflexive posturing even as an infant; he would writhe, clamp down and turn his head. I felt raw and uncomfortable all the time.

Owen stopped breastfeeding at around 11 months, which was fine with me. He was more interested in pureed food and I was gearing up to have another baby, so around that time we started feeding Owen liquids in a cup and using a spoon to feed him solids.

When Owen was ready to start solid foods, I embraced the process. I didn't buy prepared baby foods until he was much older. I made homemade purees and froze them in little ice cube trays. I made regular adult food and put full meals in the blender—pastas, beans, hummus, chunky soups—he loved savoury foods and seemed to enjoy new smells and tastes.

When Owen was two years old, he was referred to the feeding clinic—a paediatric specialty that included assessing positioning, intake, digestion and elimination—the full range of the many elements of eating that functioning adults rarely have to think about. Assessments and interventions included swallow studies, x-rays, occupational therapy, custom seating, special diets, supplements, medications and more. The conclusion the experts came to at every session was that, with intervention, Owen was more or less successfully eating by mouth and should continue to do so.

We were encouraged to continue on the path of oral feeding. The alternative was a permanent gastrostomy tube, or g-tube. I knew little of this, but it seemed to be the last resort, something a family avoids unless absolutely necessary. The interventions in Owen's case were a custom seating system (with tilt and recline) and custom head support, reflux medication, thickened fluid (using a modified corn starch), specialized utensils and cup, prescribed feeding techniques and regular home visits by a nurse to monitor breathing and lung health.

Despite all of the tips and tricks, on some mornings I was only able to feed him half a personal-size container of yogurt. This, followed by a few sips of water intended to wash it down, was then sputtered and coughed back out. He loved nibbling on crumbly crackers—this was his designated snack at nursery school. But often he would eat only half a cracker before it was time to move on to other activities.

Owen became steadily thinner. His skin became baggy and his head was noticeably bigger than the rest of his body, even taking into account the disproportionate head/body ratio typical for this age. His calorie consumption was very low and his liquid intake negligible. His bowel movements were infrequent, his stool small and hard and his urine dark yellow. His skin was sallow, and he had bags under his eyes. Many years later, looking at photos of that time, I came to see that Owen was woefully undernourished. I can see it in photos now but didn't see it then. Apparently nobody else did either.

At lunchtime Owen would arrive home, droopy and lethargic—I would lift him out of his car seat and he would fall asleep before we entered the house. Then he would wake up and eat a small meal of pureed food, choking and crying all the way through because he was so hungry.

It might seem like an easy problem to fix: just feed him more solids and give him more to drink! Not possible. His ability to chew and swallow safely was assessed repeatedly. We knew he was silently aspirating—food and fluid would slip down his airway into his lungs and pool there, becoming a perfect breeding ground for bacteria and infection. Despite our best efforts to feed him properly, Owen developed aspiration pneumonia at least once a year.

Food and thickened fluid had to be given slowly and methodically. At the last assessment before I finally threw in the towel, the instruction was to feed 1/4 teaspoon of food every 30 seconds. I calculated how long it would take to feed Owen his recommended calories and fluids: about 5 hours a day.

It was a desperate situation. Long days alone with the boys, with all activities planned around when Owen would need to eat. And it wasn't just the length of time that made things desperate. Despite the feeding techniques and tools Owen would cough, sputter, spit, vomit, choke and cry. Most of the food would end up on the floor, on his bib, or on my lap. His teeth were also in varying states of disrepair. His baby teeth had grown in jagged. Some were capped, but others were still quite sharp—a wayward bite and he would cut his lip, tongue or inner cheek.

Sometimes his high tone would interfere with eating and he would involuntarily clamp his teeth down on the rubber spoon, unable to release his jaw. A quick wriggle might get the utensil out, but many times we would have to wait for the reflex to release—his jaw would ease, the spoon would fall out and Owen's eyes would fill with tears. I am sure he, too, felt immense frustration.

One day I started to lay out all of Owen's food items in preparation for the afternoon feeding session—utensils, bowls, napkins, thickener for the liquids. Angus was an older toddler then, perhaps almost three years old. He saw what was happening and decided he wasn't going to abide it any longer. He pulled on my pant leg and said, "No!"

I was stunned. It seemed cruel. He repeated his demand and added, "Mommy. Come play."

I could see, even in my growing irritation, that he was asking me to spend time with him instead of engaging with this nonsense. As I always did, I made the best of it and found a way to involve Angus in feeding Owen. But also at that moment, I felt helpless. And hopeless. I was frustrated that I couldn't provide for either of my children properly.

❖ ❖ ❖ ❖ ❖

At my next psychotherapy session, expecting some sympathy, I spoke of the trials of feeding, the non-stop crying, the clinic encouraging me to keep going . . .

"What do you think Owen wants?"

That's a weird question. He wants what everyone wants.

"He probably wants to eat like a normal kid and I'm sure he would NOT want that thing stuck inside of him!"

"Maybe you're right. But maybe he's hungry."

I pictured my sweet boy, big wobbly head and gangly limbs, sagging skin. He's naturally skinny, that's all. I repositioned myself on the fluffy floor cushion. It was getting uncomfortable.

"You said that feeding is a struggle. That he cries all the time. That it's hard to find people who know how to feed him. You said that there is an alternative."

"Yes, yes I said that. It's all true. But that's how it is with a boy like mine. Feeding is difficult, sure. But I can't give up. He needs me to feed him."

"That last thing. Say it again."

"He needs me to feed him!" I was confused, angry. I felt tears welling. Why do these interjections always feel like a trick?

"Does he?"

I was floundering and I knew it. I mustered one last effort to save my ego: "Okay, fine, no he doesn't, but this is how people eat!"

I felt exposed. Like a fraud of a mother who can't see that her child is starving.

❖ ❖ ❖ ❖ ❖

I debated with myself for days after the session, and talked things over with Michael. He expressed relief that I was willing to consider a g-tube; he had been privately wondering how long this torture would go on.

I can't do it, I thought, because I must feed my child myself; because they said I was doing a good job; because this is how all children eat. Eating by tube is for the elderly, the terminally ill, sick babies still in the hospital. Besides, he loves flavours, textures!

It was unimaginable. But even in my resistance I could see it was becoming inevitable. I had no idea how well it would turn out.

❖ ❖ ❖ ❖ ❖

The nurse showed me the doll they use to teach older children about the procedure. It was cute—all dressed up, jaunty hat on the head.

See? The only difference is the little valve on the belly. I tried to imagine how typical children react. Maybe they think the doll is cute too. Or maybe they are horrified. Could go either way, really.

I showed the doll to Owen and he smiled.

There were a few options at the time, but the Mickey button tube was clearly the way to go. It was a small valve that would sit half in and half out of the body. The valve had a short straw which would be inserted through a surgically created hole, usually positioned somewhere just above the belly button where the stomach is situated. The end of the straw opened to the inside of the stomach and was surrounded by a deflated balloon. Once the straw was inserted through the hole, the balloon would be inflated inside the belly to act as an anchor, securing the straw in place.

The outer bit, the part that stayed outside the body, had what I thought of as a beach ball valve—a one-way opening with a tabbed closure. It also had a small port on the side, used for filling the balloon with sterile water (via a 5ml syringe) to keep it anchored. The same port was used for deflating the balloon. When the tube needed replacing, the balloon could be drained for easy removal.

"You can just do it yourself. Most parents don't need us for replacing the tube. It's super-easy!"

I held the small device in my hand. A foreign object to be forever lodged in my little boy's belly. You know how they say when someone is good at something it's like they were doing it since before they were born? I amused myself thinking that Owen was good at having foreign objects lodged in his body.

❖ ❖ ❖ ❖ ❖

I sometimes say I hated going to the hospital but it's not exactly true. We were well known in all of our clinics, the people were friendly and the cafeteria had a good salad bar and there was a Starbucks in the lobby. Everything was big and the hallways were wide and each patient room had its own bathroom. But there were two things I always dreaded: sleeping on the little bench they call a "parent bed", and bracing myself for the inevitable last-minute changes and unpleasant surprises.

❖ ❖ ❖ ❖ ❖

Twice, the g-tube procedure had been rescheduled. The postponements were particularly disappointing because once I decided to move ahead, I was focused and eager.

But on this occasion, so far so good. In the waiting room as instructed—Owen has on his gown and booties and has been fasting since last night. Owen is first on the list for the day's surgeries—a new life awaits!

The surgery itself will be simple. Poke a hole, insert the tube, throw in a stitch. The hard part will be Owen's body adjusting to the tube, which is likely to cause irritation and infection. I will also need to be trained to feed Owen, requiring one or two overnight stays in the hospital to acclimate.

"Owen's mom?" The orderly has a clipboard and is reading from a list.

"That's us! Over here!" I started to gather our things.

"There's a bit of a delay. We're going to move you to second on the list. We're looking for your file."

Owen's "file" is 6 inches thick and contained 2 folders held together with a big rubber band. How does something like that go missing?

"We only have the request form. The anaesthesiologist wants to see the whole file."

I looked at the clock. 9:20 a.m. We'd been there for more than 3 hours. I guess we can wait a bit longer.

At 10:50 a.m. another orderly with a clipboard enters.

Finally! I look around for my bag as I pull the wheelchair closer to me with my foot. Owen had fallen asleep on my lap and it was hard to move.

The orderly looks around the room. "Alex? Is Alex here?"

Who? "No, his name is Owen . . ."

"Sorry, we're still moving down the list. No file yet. We'll let you know."

I'm so hungry, and poor Owen! No food or water since last

night. This was all supposed to be finished by now. I would have already had a helping from the salad bar and a second tall mild from Starbucks. It's almost one o'clock . . .

"Owen's mom?"

Why do they never bother to find out my name? I know this game by now. I don't get up or fumble around. I barely look up from my magazine, but I raise my hand. "Here."

The nurse sits down across from me, apology oozing from her eyes with a look that says, *don't hate me, I'm just doing my job.*

"The physician who ordered the g-tube procedure signed out your son's file and may have left it in his office. Unfortunately, he's not reachable. The anaesthesiologist won't give Owen the general anaesthetic without a full history. We will have to reschedule."

I close my eyes. This can't be happening. We have been waiting for this for weeks and now we're *both* hungry.

Breathe. Open eyes. "Can I sign a waiver? Nothing bad will happen. I promise. He's been under before. " I know it doesn't work like that. But I will say anything.

"The only other option is to do the surgery without the anaesthetic. Might be safer in the long run anyway. We can freeze the skin. But he will feel the incision through the muscle and his stomach wall."

My mind is agile, I can course-correct on a dime, I am Grace Under Pressure personified, I am completely unflappable. But this doesn't compute. Surgery while conscious? I become dramatic, imagining a knife carving into the belly. He doesn't even know that he's going in for surgery. He won't have me for support. He won't even hear what's going on. They will have to hold him down. I'm angry she even suggested it and getting angrier by the minute.

"Absolutely not!"

The emotions are frothy and bubbling and taking up space and demanding attention, yet a quiet voice of reason and detached observation seeks to be heard from the depths. Something is dawning on me as my primal brain wants to fight and run at the same time.

I've been here before. Owen's been here before. We've both been poked with a sharp straw without pain relief or sleeping minds. I know how it feels and it wasn't that bad. The upside of Owen is that he doesn't anticipate, doesn't rehearse. It will be over quickly. All this waiting will be over and we can move on. What's at stake? What's most important?

"Wait."

The nurse, her message delivered and her body halfway out of her seat, pauses mid-air then slowly sits back down.

"I mean, yes. Just do it. Please tell them to do it quickly."

I could have dwelled on the suffering, the pain, the confusion. I could have imagined the trauma of Owen being held down by masked intruders with knives and bandages and rubber gloves. I knew what I was subjecting my son to and I knew that his body would remember the assault, even if his mind wouldn't go back to the moments. I knew I was responsible for what was happening and that my boy would feel pain. I knew he might wonder why I was letting this happen. I knew all of these things to be true. I also knew that I had to make a decision. I was resolute: fixing his hunger was more important than avoiding his temporary pain and my temporary stress. I sat in the waiting room, closed my eyes, and waited.

❖ ❖ ❖ ❖ ❖ ❖

When it was all over, I held my boy as close as I could, given his bandages, protruding tubes and IV lines. He didn't seem any worse for wear. As his official dinner hour approached—when I normally would have been preparing his food—I thought, for the first time, about myself. I thought, "I'm free!" Free from the food prep and the mush sputtered everywhere and the mind-numbing sameness of too many hours, every day, shoving and spooning and cajoling food into Owen. Free from the pressure and guilt of trying so bloody hard and knowing it wasn't enough. It is not an understatement to say I felt released from the bonds of slavery and servitude.

I opened a tetra-pak box of pre-made formula and, just like they showed me, poured it into the drip bottle. And I smiled.

# Thirteen

Owen had stayed in kindergarten an extra year but now he was eight and old enough for second grade, so I couldn't delay placement any longer. It was time to move up.

James Robinson was a regular public school a couple of kilometers away, near downtown Markham. It was an elementary school for typically developing children, kindergarten to Grade 8. The school also provided a program modified for disabled children from around the city, conducted in a contained classroom setting, or Community Class. Community Class was divided into junior and senior levels, each with its own staff. Sometimes they did activities together, sometimes apart. The classrooms were adapted for wheelchair access and open learning. No desks—the room was organized by activities and types of toys and devices. There was also an accessible change room and the adjoining rooms had their own direct side entrance, with a ramp.

Each child had a "buddy"—a partner from the regular school who would join the class for occasional lunchtimes or recesses. Sometimes a Community Class student would join his or her age-appropriate class for music, art or gym.

Each class had a weekly or monthly schedule which included activities in the community at large—grocery shopping and baking (classified as Life Skills), swimming, bowling, walks around the neighbourhood. There were individual lesson plans earnestly adapted and organized, but I imagined that each day took on a life of its own, bending and shifting with the moods and needs of the children.

At first I was resistant. Why, I wondered, are people with disabilities always grouped together? Why are these children bussed outside of their neighbourhoods? Why are there so many adults around here?

But I eventually relaxed into it. The staff members were kind and eager, the larger school body was engaged and sensitive and there was always a buzz of activity. The rooms were bright and cheery. Anyway, I couldn't really imagine how else this was supposed to go.

It worked, for a time. Owen had somewhere to go and other people with whom he could shape play dough, read books, feel fuzzy fabrics. And I was getting a break! Taking yoga teacher training, having lunch with friends.

I was pleased and optimistic. I even thought it was sweet when Owen won the prestigious Student of the Month award for displaying good leadership. I didn't think to ask whom he led, or to what.

❖ ❖ ❖ ❖ ❖

Over time, Community Class lost its appeal. I came to see it as makework. Babysitting. I stopped caring for the second-hand artwork that came home, the fake social constructs, the relentless cheeriness of the staff. In my darker moments, I sensed a thinly veiled agenda of looking busy and pretending—a sense I had gotten the smallest hint of years before, at nursery school.

There was an air of glossy productivity, fed by a collective do-gooder mentality that obfuscated the fact that nothing authentic was going on. I would get jolly reports of creativity, friendships, learning. How exactly are they friends, I wondered, if they are just sitting side-by-side at snack time? What does it mean, "Owen demonstrated leadership?"

I watched one day while the class blended a smoothie by taking turns with their remote on/off switches that would operate the blender; it took 5 minutes for each student to press the switch. As the one child struggled to sort himself out, cheered on by the staff, the others sat quiet and motionless. Heads slumped, eyes closed, chairs tilted back. Did they even know what was going on?

I would ask these questions and in response I would be shown more lesson plans, books, activity schedules. And working with disabled kids is perceived to be a divine calling, not like being, say, a bus driver or an office worker. Friends would say, "How wonderful Owen has somewhere to go! They must be very special people!"

What should a parent make of these earnest yet absurd conditions? And how can one say, "Yes, this is nice, but just not good enough?"

# Fourteen

Present Level: After warm-up Owen is now able to hit his switch at the appropriate time, given 1 blank square and 1 target square with 8 seconds scanning between the 2 options, with some prompts from partner (visual & auditory) allowing an average of 6-10 errors per discrete trial.

Target Goal: After warm-up Owen is now able to hit his switch at the appropriate time, given 1 blank square and 1 target square with 8 seconds scanning between the 2 options, with some prompts from partner (visual & auditory) allowing an average of 2-4 errors per discrete trial.

> Date goal was set: June 21, 2004
> Review date: August 21, 2004
> Goal Attainment Scaling Form (GAS),
> Communication and Writing Aids Service

The discussions always went around and around. I was offered options at every turn but they felt futile. I knew what I was up against. Every year, a new suggestion, a new hope.

When Owen was three: "He can use a voice-output device to communicate."

But he can't hear.

When Owen was four: "He needs to first learn cause-and-effect; learn how to use switches."

Yes, learn. Goals, checklists, spreadsheets. Time of Day/Number of Opportunities/Number of Successes. The expensive adapted toys. The battery-interrupter to adapt regular toys. The computer arranged through the Assistive Devices Program specifically for Owen's training. Games called "Press to Play" (which were really just PowerPoint animations). We tried. We really did.

When Owen was five: "It's okay if he can't hear. He just needs to know that if he pushes the button, someone will respond."

But his caregivers can't hear. I hire only deaf people. They're the only ones who sign well enough. They're the only ones who can offer consistent language input.

When Owen was six: "Then we'll attach a light signal to the switch, so they can see when he wants something."

But Owen can't see it. His head is always craned around, his chair always tilted back.

When Owen was seven: "Then we'll attach a buzzer, so he can feel when he's pushed the button."

It was enough to turn a sane woman mad.

❖ ❖ ❖ ❖ ❖

Switches are accessibility devices, relays that allow us to control electrical circuits. They turn things on and off. They regulate and adjust machines, lights, televisions. Most people manipulate switches with their hands and fingers. Light switches, remote controls, dials on the stove, mouse and keyboard. For people with disabilities, there's a whole other world of adapted switches and devices.

A button switch for a child with disabilities is small, round and brightly coloured, like a big candy, or a small indoor hockey puck. Streaming from one end like a tail is the cord, which attaches to the device you want to operate (a lamp, for example). Of course, the device itself has to be adapted to accommodate the particular kind of jack on the end of the switch cord. Or, an additional device called a switch box can be used, into which both the switch and the lamp (or whatever device you are using) can be plugged. The switch is then fastened to something the child can access easily but is sturdy enough to withstand jolts and hits and presses. Accessibility product manufacturers make devices for just this purpose—adapted computer mouse, adapted lamp, adapted CD player.

But it's not all fun and games. Switches have several modes, each useful for developing different communication, functional and cognitive skills.

- Direct mode: press for on, release for off
- Latch mode: click for on, click for off
- Timer mode: click to turn on, and the device will turn itself off after a preset period of time.

Each mode comes with its particular uses and characteristic frustrations. Latch mode was more or less useless; there was little in Owen's life that he would meaningfully operate himself that required separate on and off clicks. Also, it was confusing—the same action (pressing the switch) performed opposite functions (on and off). Direct mode—holding down the switch to operate the device - is good for driving an electric wheelchair, for example. It is not safe or desirable to just have an "On" button, or for the wheelchair to only operate for 30 seconds at a time. Instead, direct mode is like a gas pedal. It demands the user's focus and intention. Timer mode most closely simulates natural communication. A voice output device is operated in this way. Press the button, wait for the recorded voice to finish speaking, press again to initiate a new communication. Now of course, Owen couldn't hear! But we found creative uses for it anyway. We recorded a voice simply saying GO! Owen's caregiver at the time, Steve, would do a somersault every time he pressed the button. Owen would laugh hysterically, then push the button again. Simple cause and effect. It didn't matter that Owen couldn't hear it; he learned that if he pushed the button, something funny would happen.

Switch activations were the cornerstone of his therapy and activities. I was encouraged to find age-appropriate, meaningful integrations of switch-activated devices and technology. If he could master intentional switch use, he could have access to communication and language. Sounded good to me at the time. I tried everything they suggested.

❖ ❖ ❖ ❖ ❖

"Hap-py birth-day dear O-wen, hap-py birth-day to y-o-o-o-u!"

The children—Angus and a couple of neighbourhood kids—were seated around the table, eager for their cake. I had set up the switch in advance, strategically located on a hydraulic metal arm usually used to mount cameras and lighting. It was clamped to the footrest of his wheelchair and was often the source of tremendous pain when bashed into an unaware adult's kneecap. It had a small metal plate onto which I attached an industrial grade hook-and-loop fastener to hold the switch in place. The whole thing was positioned for access by Owen's foot.

I had thought a lot about this: how can an activity like blowing out a birthday candle be accessible to Owen? How can I normalize this experience—normalize *him*, really—so that the children will see he's like them, a regular kid?

Hairdryer! I'll hook it up to the switch box and plug in his button switch. HE CAN BLOW OUT HIS OWN CANDLE! Man, I'm a genius.

I had everything in place: switch, extendable metal arm with mounting bracket, switch box, hairdryer . . . I was holding the cake in both hands, cheap birthday candle burning perilously quickly. I held it up for Owen to see, fidgeting children just out of my peripheral vision.

Damn! Someone needs to help guide Owen to the switch. I put the cake down and turned Owen's wheelchair so I could reach his foot better. I didn't realize that we had already reached the end of the extension cord and that turning the wheelchair would yank the plug out of the wall.

I bent down to plug it back in and heard giggles behind me. Angus had blown out the candle.

No matter—I gently admonished Angus and lit the candle again. Okay, let's try again. "Kids, let's sing it one more time!"

". . . *dear O-wen, happy birthday to y-o-o-o-u!*" The cake was on the table with the single lit candle, hot pink wax puddling in the centre. Hairdryer pointed at the cake.

"Okay Owen! Press the button! Blow out the candle!" I tried to communicate this with one hand, signing.

Owen looked at me pensively. His chin was red and scraped from the "chin prompt" which was attached to his headrest. The theory behind the chin prompt is that when something is placed under the chin, a floppy head might be triggered to lift itself. Owen's floppy head didn't know this. Instead, he would push down into it, rubbing his chin raw on the neoprene. I used bandanas and cloth napkins to separate his skin from the plastic but when he drooled, he made everything wet and slimy, making the friction burns worse.

To give him relief, I would remove the chin prompt and tilt his chair back. If he was relaxed, he would nestle back into the chair and sit comfortably. If he was excited or tense, he would flail like a turtle on its back. Either way, if he was tilted back—like now—he couldn't see what was happening.

"Hang on guys! Owen can't see!" I put the hairdryer down, reattached his chin prompt and used the lever on the back of his chair to tip him up again. This meant the metal supporting arm for the switch also had to be repositioned.

I was starting to get hot and agitated. Why can't anything be simple? We were turning into a circus act.

The three-year-olds were getting restless.

"When can we have cake?"

"I want the flower!"

"I get the strawberry!"

I held the hairdryer up to the cake with one hand and used my other hand to guide Owen's foot to the switch. Usually I would coach, encourage and wait patiently. Not this time. With his ankle in my hand, I pressed the bottom of his foot onto the switch and the hairdryer sparked to life, blowing hot air at the cake and puffing out the candle. Pink wax streaked across the cake.

Owen looked mildly amused. I let out a sigh. The kids were already digging out the sugary flowers.

I put down the hairdryer and picked up the knife to cut the cake.

❖ ❖ ❖ ❖ ❖

The professionals anticipated Owen's potential communication difficulties from the beginning. He was assessed a few years earlier, in nursery school.

"His deafness will be his biggest problem."

I looked at Owen's splayed body on the floor mat, legs in typical frog position, head cranked to the left. Hardly, I thought. Are we looking at the same boy?

"We should start to think about language. Choice-making. Initiating communication."

I supposed she was right but it seemed early. What two-year-old does those things anyway?

Most, it turns out. Children typically make hundreds of choices every day; express all kinds of things; seek or demand attention. And they use their bodies and their developing expressive language to do so. They don't need to be *taught* language—they spontaneously use it every day, right from the beginning. But I didn't know this yet.

"Oh, I'm sure he'll communicate with me when he's ready!"

"How . . . ? Does he babble? Say words?" Either she was giving me the benefit of the doubt or humouring me.

Okay, fine. No. But I can tell what he wants! He's my son after all. I said, "We're learning sign language . . ."

"So, he uses his hands a little . . . ?"

I was getting exasperated. "No, he doesn't use his hands . . ."

"Kids with disabilities need a system. A consistent, clear means of making choices, expressing themselves, telling stories."

I didn't get what she was talking about. In fact, I was feeling irritated. How can you possibly teach something to a boy who can't do anything, who is unable even to hear or move intentionally?

I had, they pointed out, been at this for only a few years and Owen is still a child—Rome wasn't built in a day. They encouraged me:

"One step at a time!"

"Keep going."

"Don't give up."

"There is always a way in."

❖ ❖ ❖ ❖ ❖

I hold up one of Owen's board books so he can see. It has rigid pages and bright pictures. I sign the story to Owen, book tucked under my chin, shifting and adjusting as I move. Miming like a clown. Owen watches out of the corners of his eyes—he has this unfortunate affliction the effect of which is that he can't look directly at the thing he wants to see. Reflex pulls his head to one side so he can only see things peripherally. So, fine. I've learned not to chase his line of vision because he will only look away again.

Signing: "Look! Dog! Brown cute. Eats, what? Apple! Red round."

Owen's line of vision remains directed upward and to the left, disinterested in the book or incapable of casting his eyes down. In fact, he never looked down. Had to pull his whole head forward to see anything below mid-horizon.

Page 1 done. Signing: "Look again! See?" Pan slowly. Put book down. "Owen? Do you want MORE? More book? Yes? Press the button! Here (taps foot). Press the button! Next what? Light on! Bzzzzz! More book? Press!" Hands come down, communication stops. Wait.

Watching carefully, I see that Owen's big toe is wiggling. But his reflexes are opposing him, as they almost always do. If he wants to hold something, his hand shoots open with flat fingers and a wide palm. If he wants to let go, his fist clenches so tight he gets fingernail marks in his palm. Wants to look left, head flings right. In this moment, his thighs are rigid with heels pressed back into the back wall of the custom-made footrest on his wheelchair, padded to prevent self-injury. He's pressing back to stabilize. Movement of the toe is isolated, scanning back and forth like radar, searching for a switch to press. Then I see the problem: the switch is too far. Slowly I move it closer. Set him up for success, they said. Bring it to where the toe can reach. Owen is sweating, hands are clenched, elbows wrenched back and shoulders thrust forward like chicken wings. Switch is within reach! He rubs the outer edge of the switch with his toe, getting his bearings, preparing for the big push forward.

"More book? Story continue? Press! Press!" More sweating. Is that anxiety in the creases of his eyes? I wonder what he's thinking.

"Good job! Working hard! Press, Owen! More story? Yes?!" I'm getting into it now. Any minute we will see that Owen can think! Respond! Engage!

Something clicks—message from brain to toe travels like a shot from a cannon. Toe scrunches back, tucked knee straightens, previously flexed ankle now extends. Big toe rockets towards the switch, knocking it to the floor, jamming the front of the toe into the side of the metal support bracket.

Owen has stubbed his toe, slightly tearing the toenail. The switch is dangling from its cord, light and buzzer hopelessly, shamefully, quiet. Owen exhales, limbs soften and go limp, head slumps.

I hold his bare foot in my hand, looking in his eyes. We both have tears, although only his are rolling down his face. You wanted more, didn't you Owen?

"Good job! Press? Yes!"

I reposition the switch. I pick up the book, turn the page, and continue the story.

❖ ❖ ❖ ❖ ❖

What was all this for? To give him a sense of independence, so he can indicate that he needs something. This was to be the foundation upon which to build more advanced communication skills, so he can direct his own care, so he can engage in meaningful conversations and relationships.

I appreciated the importance of this effort. It wouldn't always be "pick this or that," "is this red or blue," "stop or go," "yes or no." Language is about moving towards abstraction—the more abstract, the more sophisticated, the more civilized. Feelings, desires, memories, metaphors. An ability to move beyond the concrete. To do more than point—to analyze, process, interpret, conclude. But I was overwhelmed by questions and persistent doubts. What if I know we'll never get there? What if I'm certain? Who would I dare tell? Who would listen? And who would dare agree? Are we all supposed to die trying? And why do we always have to be working on something?

Is *hope* the only thing that matters?

❖ ❖ ❖ ❖ ❖

I had requested a meeting of Owen's team members and all groups were represented: Early Intervention, York Region District School Board, speech-language pathologists, even the EC Drury School for the Deaf. The living room was full.

We were trying to piece together an educational trajectory for Owen. He was enrolled in school but I had requested that the focus there be social, not academic. So we were developing a home-based program for his communication and language development. This was exceedingly difficult given Owen's physical disabilities and profound level of hearing loss.

Deaf people (who sign) rely on motor skills to communicate. Physically disabled people with a limited capacity for intentional movement rely on auditory input/output and technology to communicate. Owen was stuck in the middle, a full member of neither group. We could not harness a single thing—eye gaze, pointing, switches, vocalizing—to good and consistent effect.

We had to pick something to focus on and we had decided that his foot was our best bet. His leg was easier to stabilize than his arm, and his toes seemed to have more dexterity and intentional movement. For months we worked on improving his toe-pressing action, rigging up a signaling device close to his foot. He couldn't hear the auditory signals confirming that he did indeed press it, so we attached a buzzer and a bright light.

They asked, "How is it going?"

I thought about our failed attempts; the many hours we worked so persistently and got nothing back; the abandoned play kits; the half-filled log sheets; the little lies I told myself about Owen's progress to keep me engaged; the persistent hopefulness of the therapists; the boredom of Owen's caregivers as they trudged through the therapy sessions. I briefly considered telling them that that is how it's going, but they did come all this way—and maybe we're just around the corner from success! Maybe things will shift.

"Good," I said. "We're working through the communication goals."

They nodded, made notes, looked pleased.

The dialogue meandered. They spoke of more tactics, more strategies. Discussions ensued of educational plans, types of support, assistance required. An example was raised: How to teach colours—RED, let's say. How will we teach RED? Sorting objects into buckets, dressing in RED clothes, matching a colour card to RED objects, showing RED things when outdoors. We can have a colour of the week! Identify RED when eating, dressing, at therapy. So many ideas for teaching RED . . .

This went on for many minutes. I looked from face to face, hearing but not listening. I had one of those occasional moments in which I am hovering above the room, eavesdropping on them and myself. Everything sounds stupid, wrong. I feel irritated and superior. A bad combination in a room of good intentions and detailed lesson plans.

I interjected into the group's lively debates: "He can see when something is red."

Eyes turn to me. The mom is speaking!

"If he can see it, and I see he sees it, why does he have to "say" it?"

Awkward silence. Colluding gazes meet each other across the room. What is this now? Have they misread me? Have they taken my eagerness at face value and assumed I was on board? Was I now somehow against them? Are they no longer sure that I understand how this works? The experts weighed in patiently:

"So we know what he understands . . ."

"So he can express preferences . . ."

"As a foundation for language development . . ."

"So he can learn along with peers in his age group . . ."

"So we can measure his progress . . ."

Who can argue with that? Still, I wanted to bonk their heads together. Look: the reality of it is that the boy can't do anything and probably never will. I love him no less for it—but that's the truth.

# Fifteen

Some research reports that as many as 80% of couples who have children with disabilities eventually break up.

Raising a child with a disability is really hard work. It opens philosophical divides, creates financial burdens, steals any free time parents of young children don't really have anyway and contributes to a level of fatigue and lack of self-care that no couple can survive unscathed. And what of the emotional stress, the fear of the future, the self-criticism, the blame of the other?

When acquaintances learn that Owen's dad and I are not together anymore they pull their lips tight across their faces and nod knowingly. Eyebrows furrow. Yes, they think. It must have been so hard.

It was. But that's not why we split up.

There were occasional frustrated silences and clenched teeth, but no fights. Sure, Owen was the focal point of the family, the point around which our household's attentions orbited, but Owen was rarely the subject of disagreement or even discussion. There were no heart-to-hearts concerning "what do we do" and "what's next." Owen's management was mostly my domain. I was in charge of his care and I did my job well. Michael was an engaged family man and a willing supporting player in Owen's management, offering guidance and opinions when asked. For his part, Michael worked a serious job, earned good money and paid the bills, participating happily when requested and happy to withdraw when I had things under control. We rarely argued, didn't raise our voices, didn't hang up in anger. We were a productive, companionable partnership. We glided. We glided through, around, near. We were a well-oiled machine operating largely without any friction. Or spark.

❖ ❖ ❖ ❖ ❖

When Owen started kindergarten in Markham I became a yoga teacher and built a small business teaching classes in friends' basements. I ordered food boxes from organic delivery services, stopped drinking alcohol and stopped eating sugar. I took up running. I probably looked happy but never stopped to ask myself if I actually was.

The truth was that we were bored. We had become passionless and uninteresting. We would go out to dinner on a rare "date night", eat Indian food, talk about lifeless things and go home early. We entertained ourselves with television, couples therapy and accumulating things—cars and a boat and an apartment building. Conversations were amiable, controlled, humourless. We immersed ourselves in family life, enjoying our boys and our acquisitions, but rarely noticing each other.

If we were to have shed our defences and started talking, what would we have said to each other?

I might have admitted to feeling like I was suffocating, like this can't be all there is and that I never wanted to move to Markham anyway. I would have mentioned, maybe, that I had completely lost any sense of lust or desire and I couldn't remember the last time I actually wanted to have sex. (Then, again, I might not have bothered to say anything because Michael could surely tell anyway.) I might have said I feel like a pathetic stereotype. I might have said, I thought I was going to be great.

And Michael? What stories of his went unuttered? Perhaps he would have told me what he was thinking the night the silence got so bad I punched a hole in the wall beside the guest bathroom, which he patched up neatly the next day and which neither of us mentioned again although we could still see where the paint covered the plaster after everything dried.

Maybe he would have said, "I didn't want this either, and whatever happened to us, anyway?" Maybe our faith in each other wouldn't have eroded to the point that the gulf between us grew too wide, trust was questioned, feelings were suppressed, truths went unspoken.

What if we had taken the signs seriously and had decided it was time to show up for each other—to be curious and protective and vulnerable? A year before the split, our therapist said we were in the valley of despair, that he feared for us, that we were headed for trouble if we didn't wake up.

We didn't believe it. We would look at each other across our big living room, over the heads of our beautiful boys, squinting through the beams of afternoon sun that would shine into our eyes through the big picture window, barely blocked by the trellis of the deck we had recently built, and thought that if this is despair, we're doing okay!

I suppose one could say that Owen had a role in our break-up—as did our location, our distractions, our lack of interest in each other, our benign neglect, our very natures as individuals, and everything else under the sun that came before the moment I said "I'm leaving." It all somehow contributed and yet not one thing stands out as the main reason. An old joke: everyone dies of the same thing—the heart stops beating.

# Sixteen

When Michael and I were living together, there was an ongoing question as to where Owen should sleep. He had a small bed in our bedroom but he rarely slept there. Whoever rocked Owen to sleep in the night was usually too tired to bother easing him into his own bed and tiptoeing away. It was futile anyway; Owen would inevitably wake, either immediately as he was put down or a very few minutes later. He would fling himself awake, stare bug-eyed at the ceiling and whimper until he was retrieved and re-cuddled back to sleep. So instead, whoever was holding him when he fell asleep would just bring him into our bed. I admit it was a little crowded.

Sometimes Owen would stay asleep in his own bed, but it would take a lot of work. It went like this: Once he was asleep in my arms, I would slowly lower us both onto his toddler bed, jiggling and rocking all the way down. I would lie in his bed with him then, after a few minutes, slowly drop one leg over the side, then slither the rest of my body down to the floor, carefully sliding my trapped arm out from under his torso. Having quietly dropped to the floor on my belly, I would crawl out in the hopes he wouldn't see or sense my shadow moving on the wall. If Michael was near the doorway, I would wave one hand wildly to shoo him away and whisper loudly, "Go back! He's asleep! Don't creak the floor!"

Michael was pragmatic about sleep. It was as vital as eating and drinking and if Owen was going to be awake anyway, he could do it in another room. We had many discussions about migrating Owen out of our bedroom, but I was adamant.

When I moved out and found my own place to live, it was a relief to not have to argue about where Owen would sleep. In our new apartment, Owen always slept in my bed, or right beside my bed in a smaller toddler bed elevated on plastic bed-raisers to bring him to my level. There was just enough space between our beds for me to dangle my legs while seated on the edge of my mattress so I could reach his feeding pump, adjust his position, or scoop him up and heave him into my bed in the middle of the night.

On most nights, he started out in his own bed, but morning would inevitably find us curled up together in my bed, always in the same position. I found a way to keep him tucked into a ball without having to sit up; spooning, Owen facing out, my knees tucked into the backs of legs, his head resting on one of my arms, my other arm draped over his hip and torso. This position ensured continual, evenly distributed pressure on much of his body, calming his dystonia and allowing him to sleep.

The catch? I couldn't sleep like this. My arm would fall asleep. I would get uncomfortable from his body heat. I would need to stretch and move without waking him. I developed chronic pain in one shoulder and the opposite hip from years of lying in this position, barely asleep. Of course he would need to stretch and move as well—if left to his own devices he would fling himself awake or roll onto his face. So I would lie awake, willing myself to fall asleep but really just waiting until he roused slightly so I could readjust myself as well.

He would also pee in the night, sometimes through his diaper, soaking the bed. Or his overnight water drip would become dislodged and I would scoop him up out of his bed to discover he was drenched with water. Or he would cough and choke and need suctioning. Other times, things would just fall apart for no apparent reason maybe because I was too tired or he would be too fidgety or both. When he was overtired and sensed my impatience, he would pout and whimper. These were moments when I was not at my best. I would look at him and think, "It's you or me, kid."

My body had become accustomed to this routine, although I

suspect I was functioning far below par. When nights got bad, I would bring Owen out to the living room, turn on the TV, arrange his cushions and blankets, then go back to the bedroom and close the door.

I wanted to be more patient. I wanted to love him and cuddle him and be gentle with him and soothe him back to sleep. But sometimes, I just couldn't do it. That one more whine or whimper or twitch would put me over the edge. I came up against my limits as a human being. It was like torture, the restlessness and constant demand for adjustment in the middle of the night.

Fatigued and irritated, I would hoist him in my arms, mustering every reserve in my body and soul to keep myself from squeezing him too tightly or moving him gruffly. I would expel my energy by stomping as I plodded my way down the hall with Owen in my arms, walking loudly to make a statement. I didn't care who it woke — it felt good to release the tension.

My apartment was a 3-bedroom unit on the main floor of a large North Toronto home. A large bay window in one wall of the spacious living room faced a quiet residential street. This time of night was dark and quiet. Kneeling down, I would balance Owen on one leg and, braced by one arm, I would feel around for the U-shaped baby pillow and stack of blankets, carefully arranging them while trying not to drop Owen. I could then grasp the remote control; the television would emit a static-y buzzing sound as it leaped to life, temporarily blinding us both.

Because his reflexes would pull his body in the direction opposite the one in which he wished to go, Owen couldn't look at the television — or, for that matter, at any other object — directly. When watching TV, he would strain to keep his eyes tuned to the screen even as his head was pulling around the other way.

Watching TV in a mirror, strangely, was the antidote. I would position Owen between the TV and a mirror—the mirror propped on the floor and tilted just right for the TV to be displayed in his view. He would start by looking at the TV but then as soon as something interesting happened—like someone walking, an object moving, text appearing—his head would whip away from the TV. A second or two, and his eyes would again find the TV in the mirror and all would be well. On the rare occasion he couldn't maintain the excitement of that view either, he would settle exactly in the middle—eyes fixed on the ceiling and the action happening on both sides, perceived through "Spidey senses" and peripheral vision.

In the middle of the night, though, with the combination of exhaustion and painful glare of the screen, there would be little neck-wrenching excitement. Instead, Owen was a bag of bones. Relieved, maybe, of the bedroom tussle and my irritation, he would be floppy and loose. His eyes usually remained closed until he adjusted to the dark.

Sometime shortly after his rather unloving descent and placement on the floor and the rushed rearrangement of his limbs, I would notice his helplessness and vulnerability. I suppose it was nature's way of ensuring that I didn't abandon him.

Before returning to bed I would conduct this ritual: I would get down on my knees, hunch over his broken, tired body and I would run both of my hands through his thick, curly hair, root to tip. Then, I would cup his face in my hands as I leaned in to kiss his forehead. I felt a love for Owen that I almost couldn't bear. I would think: I'm so sorry Owen. So sorry I have to leave you like this; so sorry I wasn't gentle with you; so sorry that I can't do more.

# Seventeen

> Owen's mother reported that approximately 4 months ago his tone began to increase in both the upper and lower limbs. His tone was so high that he was sometimes breaking off pieces from his wheelchair and was unable to sleep at night . . . [The doctor] has discussed the possibility of a baclofen pump in the future given Owen's significant hypertonia and this possibility was again discussed today given the high dose of oral baclofen that Owen is taking in light of this most recent episode of increased tone.
>
> **Pediatric Rehabilitation Clinic, November 23, 2006**

The baclofen pump is an implanted device that delivers liquid medication directly into the spinal fluid. The medication is kept in a reservoir inside a puck-shaped device. That device also contains the pump mechanism and a battery. The whole assembly is inserted just under the skin, above the hipbone. A catheter or tube runs out one side of the pump, winds around to the back of the inside of the body and follows up along the spine. Based on a number of factors, the neurosurgeon determines at what point in the spinal column it should be inserted—the closer to the brain, the more widespread the effect on the whole body. The end of the catheter is inserted into the intrathecal space in the spine (the vertical section of spinal column that holds the cerebral-spinal fluid) and held in place by a stitch or two.

The surgeon makes a large incision into the belly to insert the device and a smaller incision in the lower back so he can thread the catheter up the spine.

❖ ❖ ❖ ❖ ❖

When the pump was first implanted in Owen, it was filled with saline. Once his body became accustomed to the device, the doctor replaced the saline with medication. Over the course of the next few months, we visited the outpatient clinic to have the dose increased slowly, attending appointments once or twice a week. It took about six months of increases to reach an appropriate and useful level of baclofen infusion.

Changing the dose of the medication or refilling the reservoir requires special training. The pump itself is fully enclosed in the body but is remotely "accessible" through a scanner-like machine that can take readings and send new messages. The handheld scanner, when positioned over the device, can monitor and transmit through the skin.

Of course, refilling the medication reservoir is not a remotely controlled activity. The device has a small medication entry port, which is palpable through the skin. The physician can tell exactly at which point to insert the syringe, through the skin and into the medication port. Once refill is complete, the device is programmatically updated through the scanner.

❖ ❖ ❖ ❖ ❖

Baclofen is a medication often prescribed to relieve spasticity. Spasticity is not just muscle cramping from activity or exertion—rather, spasticity is a neurological disorder that causes muscles to tighten. Massage and external therapies can relieve the pain and discomfort, but they don't stop the incorrect messages sent from the brain to the limbs. Baclofen works to reduce these faulty brain transmissions. It also has a sedating effect—as one neurologist told me, "Yes, we can medicate away spasticity. It's called 'general anaesthetic.' "

Unfortunately, Owen had two conditions, each of which sometimes exacerbated the other: spasticity and dystonia. Spasticity made his muscles rigid and tight, whereas dystonia, a neurological disorder related to movement, made his movements uncoordinated and often uncontrollable. If he wanted to reach for something, he would have to overcome his arm's tendency to wave and circle out of control. The baclofen, prescribed for the spasticity, didn't help the dystonia.

There are few medical treatments available to treat dystonia. The one we would eventually consider—deep brain stimulation—had not yet surfaced as a viable option. And his spasticity seemed to be the worse of the two problems. We would need to deal with first things first.

Owen's dystonic movements could be reduced somewhat with direct physical pressure and containment of the limb or body part. Pressure on the shoulder would stop the arm from shaking. Bending him at the hips and cradling him like a baby would relieve the overall, full-body thrusting. Effective, yes. But a lot of work. Owen's dystonia and spasticity would continue in his sleep. Movement and tightness would prevent him from falling asleep or would wake him in the night. Baclofen helped make him very sleepy, but it suppressed his breathing/coughing response, so his medication dosing required careful monitoring and ongoing assessment.

Our hope was that the baclofen pump would administer the medication efficiently with acceptably few side effects, helping calm Owen's body for better sleeping, ease of positioning and improved function.

❖ ❖ ❖ ❖ ❖

Although the appointment had been bumped a couple of times, the eventual timing of the surgery was perfect. We scheduled my move out of the family home at the same time. Owen emerged from the hospital two weeks after his surgery, ready to start a new life.

❖ ❖ ❖ ❖ ❖

Owen's body was so small that the baclofen pump stuck out like an appendage. The outline of the hockey puck-sized device could be seen and felt through the skin, nestled snugly in the space between his right hipbone and lower ribs. If you put your ear to it, you could hear it ticking.

I would never have admitted to regretting putting it in. Indeed, I had pushed for it, thought it a good preventive measure. And it did help; Owen was softer, looser, he slept more. Actually, slept much more . . . Still, I was deeply conflicted. There were many reasons: the permanence of the device; the invasiveness of the surgery; the ugly scars and unpleasant post-op infection. But more than these reasons—I felt I had crossed a line. Owen was sleepy all the time and when awake, his alertness and capacity to engage seemed greatly diminished. And I wasn't actually sure we had relieved any of his suffering. I wasn't sure he ever *was* suffering at all. I pondered an uncomfortable thought: anecdotally, I knew of or read about people who had opted out of particular treatments because they would rather not medicate away their personality or their lucidity or their ability to take in the world. Would Owen have been one of them? Would he have chosen this for himself?

I had gotten what I wanted—he was easier to manage. And I was sorry. I felt my regret most keenly on those occasions that we returned home from the clinic after having had the amount of medication adjusted. The regret followed me around day and night. I transmitted my regret to Owen every night while he slept.

I like to imagine that he knew this, and forgave me.

# Eighteen

Critics of corporate life have identified a workplace phenomenon: Fake Work. Fake, because it creates the illusion of productivity when the activities actually don't contribute to the production of anything real or meaningful. Even metrics are a red herring—arbitrary and random measures that serve to make us spin our wheels faster and justify our own existence to ourselves and to each other.

I encountered Fake Work in the disability world. Institutions and therapists like disabled kids and their families to be working on stuff, to be improving, to have goals and accomplishments. To be all they can be! This persistent striving can create an environment where Fake Work is prevalent and even encouraged.

The years of communication and physical therapy felt like this, like an endless stream of appointments filled with pep talks, encouraging observations, research reports, new directions, good intentions; while Owen sat bored, overmedicated, under-involved. I would leave appointments with plans, papers, binders, arrive home and add them to the pile of similar documents I had already accumulated. I would hire someone to look after Owen while I pored over the notes—prioritizing, logging, scheduling, making follow-up appointments.

Everything was full: the shelves of my bookcase were full, the slots in my accordion folder were full, our appointment book was full, my brain was full. All in service of our goals for Eating-Swallowing-Sitting-Listening-Language Comprehension-Alternative and Augmentative Communication-Socializing-Sleeping-Bowel Movements.

At every turn I was faced with a Herculean task. Random goals, from memory:

- Lift head
- Count
- Match colours
- Sort
- Initiate activity
- Choose yes
- Choose no
- Choose yes or no
- Choose from 2 options
- Choose from 3 options
- Swallow without choking
- Sleep through the night
- Press the button at the right time
- Press the button to say something
- Press the button to turn on the lights, the fan, the remote control car, the blender . . .

I want to cringe, cry, yell when I think of my thirty-something self. I worked so hard, and yet underneath it all I felt the futility. "Come on Owen! You can do it!" But I would be thinking to myself: Forget it, he will never do it, he hates this stuff anyway; just give it up. I could pick just one thing of the fifty and do only that one thing for ten years and it would still never be done. It's all too much, and it will never be enough.

❖ ❖ ❖ ❖ ❖

I met Owen's first speech-language pathologist when Owen was at nursery school. Over the years, we became friends. No longer Owen's immediate therapist, she was now my trusted advisor, collaborator and confidante. Eight years after our first meeting, I told her, I give up. I am not doing this anymore. I have nothing left.

She wondered what happened along the way. Did we burn you out? Surely there is more work to be done? Surely there is still potential?

I wrote her this email:

*My apparent abandonment of AAC (Alternative and Augmentative Communication) has nothing to do with my acceptance of Owen himself—it's more about my exhaustion and what I'm seeing as futility. I do wish he could communicate and I wish I could give that to him—but at what cost?*

*Owen loves language and switches and cause/effect and anything that gives him some sort of control or understanding of his world. My chief motivation for getting the baclofen pump was not actually about the spasticity in its own right. It was to see if we could support him to gain more function so that switches/AAC were not so difficult for him to use. The hope of that went out the window with removing the pump—and, honestly, the amount of baclofen he required to calm him down enough to access switches actually made him so dopey he had no capacity to enjoy or understand what was happening*

*My (our?) will and desire to help and support Owen is so strong it's easy to ride the wave of all that we know about whatever perspective we're approaching him from. But, now, after all these years, it feels like such a trap and a set-up for failure. No matter what I do, it will never be enough. Which is not to say that I should do nothing! It means that I should pick my battles and do what I can. I feel like I'm just trying to keep him alive and keep the household engine chugging.*

*I think if it's about acceptance, it's about accepting reality—not about accepting Owen "for who he is," as though he doesn't need or shouldn't get as much support as possible—and accepting my own human limitations around working so, so hard on one important but small area of his life. Owen's needs compete so heavily with everyone else's, including my own. How do I begin to figure it all out?*

And, perhaps this is only justifying my own choices, but I don't assume that Owen is living a lesser life because he doesn't have a communication system. Well, okay, maybe I do assume that—but he's also living a lesser life because he can't walk or eat or talk or use the toilet or sing or dance—all the things that we equate with living a quality, independent life.

As far as your role is concerned, you hold an immense place in my heart for your support, candour and encouragement. You could never have known my own internal stresses or dialogues or justifications because I would always wear my shining-hero cape whenever you came over. Over the years I began to understand that you (and other professionals) only had one piece of the puzzle and I didn't expect you to have all the answers. Surely by now you know how much I value your input and opinions and experience! But that doesn't mean I act on them. Owen's current lack of communication is assuredly not a result of your or others' ineffectual interventions or suggestions. I did try them all, and none of them felt right, or were too hard to implement. Which is all about Owen and me, not you or the systems.

I guess the question is: am I supposed to keep searching until we find the right one (communication system)? Am I supposed to keep at it until one of them works? And back to my original question—at what cost?

*J.J.*

# Nineteen

> Owen has been exposed to a variety of activities and discussions related to our unit on "Space." We are learning about the patterns of change observable on earth as a result of the movement of the different bodies in the solar system.
>
> Owen has continued to learn about First Nation peoples and European explorers. He was also exposed to the theories related to the origin of the Aboriginal Peoples (e.g. migration and settlement).
>
> **Excerpts, Provincial Report Card, March 31, 2008**

After our separation, Michael and I each eventually moved back downtown, and I was eager for Owen to join a school program. I needed time to adjust to my new life and get Angus settled into his new school and new routines.

Toronto has only segregated schools for kids like Owen. Rather than enrol Owen in a segregated program, I tried to enrol him in a school for the deaf. Unfortunately, deafness combined with his level of disability is very difficult to manage. To be manageable he had to be only one or the other. It was impossible for us to pretend he wasn't disabled. It was much easier to pretend he's not deaf.

The school was a short bus ride away into the leafy, upscale residential neighbourhood of Lawrence Park. On the school tour, I noted the beauty of the area; hilly walks, interesting ravines. How nice for the kids!

"No, they don't go out," the teacher said. "The kids stay inside."

A rush of nostalgia came over me as I walked the smooth, composite marble floors, peeked in the rooms and saw the familiar cinderblock walls, gazed at the we're-all-different-but-really-we're-all-the-same messages and images on the bulletin boards.

But unlike the classrooms of my own schooldays, these had six students each, attended by a teacher, two or three assistants, volunteers, therapists, nurses. In most instances, the number of adults equalled in number or outnumbered the students. There was a change room with an adult-sized changing table, a nursing station for administration of meds and supplies and a large cafeteria laid out to accommodate wheelchairs.

From the hallway, the classrooms sounded like hives of activity. Conversations, music, clatter; even laughter!

During the tour, we were allowed to peek in on a class or two. Hang on: those sounds were not coming from the students. It was the staff. The adults were talking over the students' heads. Most of the kids were just sitting quietly.

Naturally the adults will have cause to talk to each other throughout the day: to communicate to run the classroom, get activities going, collaborate on plans. They will need to talk to the students, to run their programmes, to sing. Of course.

And yet . . .

As we were escorted through the halls of the school for the rest of our tour I felt an overwhelming sense of despair. I can't describe exactly what was wrong or why throughout the whole tour I was holding back tears. The walls were bright, some of the teachers were young and keen, some of the students were up and about doing what students do. I can only say that, during that first visit, I was utterly disheartened. Beyond the buzz, I sensed an environment devoid of connection, authenticity and learning. The place looked like a school but it didn't feel like one; it felt like a facility in which employees looked after disabled kids, more institutional and soulless than any other place Owen and I had been.

I was so sad because this was his only schooling option. And it felt like a glimpse of an unavoidable, institutional future.

❖ ❖ ❖ ❖ ❖

It was a bad winter. Owen was in the lull between adjusting to the newly implanted baclofen pump and crashing into an oncoming health crisis that would change everything. There were many days of school skipped due to Owen's appointments and precarious health, bus mix-ups, class assistants on vacation, teachers sick. Sometimes the teacher would call me to let me know that she was understaffed; that I could still bring Owen to school if I wanted *but*, she was careful to add, she would be very busy as she would be alone with all the kids.

I certainly didn't mind keeping Owen home from school as long as I could find support for a few hours. It was physical work but emotional relief. I hated putting him on the bus every morning, knowing where he was going. In my twelve years with Owen, this was the stretch of time I came closest to feeling depressed.

❖ ❖ ❖ ❖ ❖

One day, the bus wasn't running because it had snowed heavily overnight and the streets were still covered. I wouldn't otherwise have brought Owen to school, but he was restless and cranky and I really needed a nap; we hadn't slept well the night before and I knew that none of his caregivers were available until evening. And if Owen was going to continue to be unhappy, he could easily do so at school until I was rested.

I called the school and they assured me that indeed it was open and I was welcome to bring Owen in myself. I bundled up all three of us, scraped the ice and snow from the top of the van and loaded up the boys. We then embarked on the slow but pleasant drive up to the school.

The front door of the school has a wide overhang protecting a long circular drive. Usually, buses and parents pull up to the front of the school, let out the children to waiting staff and volunteers then continue on their way. Daily parking for staff and visitors is accommodated by a large parking lot just to the side of the school. I'll just pull in there, I thought. I had a side-entry van with a lowered floor, and needed adequate clearance to open the door, engage the ramp, and wheel Owen out.

I had it all planned out as I turned on to the street and wound my way up to the school. I drove along slowly, surprised to see so many cars in the circular drive. It was easily 100 meters long and was filled with cars parked bumper to bumper. Good thing there was a parking lot on the other side of the school.

As I turned the van into the driveway I saw the mound of snow in front of us, blocking the entrance to the lot. I stopped and looked; yes, the entire area was covered in at least 2 feet of snow and the street snowplow had piled up a mountain at the entrance leaving no access to the lot.

I found a clear residential driveway just beyond and used it to make a 3-point turn back to the driveway at the school. I thought, "Surely the staff members' cars have not completely plugged things up. Surely I can still get in."

Alas, no. The cars were, in fact, parked 2-deep in the driveway—a feat that could have been accomplished only if someone had actually directed traffic and organized the cars as they were coming in.

I drove home, frustrated boys in the back of the van, preparing the speech I would deliver to the unsuspecting secretary who thought she was going to have an easy day without students.

It was my turn to be surprised when she said, "But the staff have nowhere else to park!"

❖ ❖ ❖ ❖ ❖

Owen had a friend at that school. Or at least, he had a fan. A classmate, a girl about 3 years older. She seemed to adore him. She learned some signs, helped him with his blanket and coat on cold days, wanted to accompany him everywhere. She could walk, utter phrases, do things. She was physically capable and significantly developmentally delayed.

I wished we could have had a conversation in private. I would have asked, "Are you happy here? Are they nice to you? Do you trust them?"

❖ ❖ ❖ ❖ ❖

I didn't have a name for the uneasiness I felt with the school. Of course there were some obvious criticisms: simulated productivity, lack of meaningful experiences and exchanges, the never-ending pretending. All of it needed to go—but these weren't the immediate dangers.

I eventually realized what was missing. In Owen's other environments, there was a natural transparency and accountability. I was invited in, I participated, I could bear witness to all that went on. And even more importantly, there were others around—students, parents—who could attest to the work being done and actions being taken. There was an inbuilt self-regulation because there were participants and witnesses capable of sharing and comparing their experiences.

In contrast this school was a closed book. Bus in, bus out. I wasn't refused entry, but in comparison to what I had experienced previously, parents seemed to be welcome by invitation only. With the exception of the handful of typically developing "community" kids who were integrated into a pilot program, all of the students were significantly disabled and many of them could not communicate independently.

This facility and many others like it require the parents' utter trust in the people, the program and the system to deliver on their promises, to regulate themselves and to report their own offences. How could I be sure this would ever happen? I had no cause to be suspicious. I also had no reason to trust.

Perhaps I am overstating my case. Perhaps it is hysterical thinking that leads me to believe that these children, who are extremely vulnerable and unable to speak for themselves, should not be put into these institutional settings or warehoused together. Maybe it's unreasonable to think that a school's primary focus should not be the convenience of the teachers and administration. Maybe it's too much to ask that a school for severely disabled children should be set up to serve the children in a dignified, inclusive and genuinely meaningful way; maybe it's wrong to criticize a system that makes up for poor execution with good intentions.

But I don't think so.

# Twenty

Our move from Markham to Toronto meant that we would be located in a different administrative region of healthcare and home services. New caseworkers, new agencies, new funding programs. Although we had moved a year earlier we had only recently begun a contract with a local agency to provide Personal Support services. We had already been receiving support services for a few weeks, but they still required a home visit with the manager.

The manager showed up with little hospital booties—and a nametag, and an agency t-shirt—and insisted that the caregiver wear them too. He reminded the caregiver to wear rubber gloves when filling the g-tube bottle or giving medication or using the suction machine.

I found this offensive; my home was not an institution. I gave medication with my bare hands all the time. When Owen was choking on his own mucous, I worked quickly to pull his head forward and get the long suction tube in his mouth. Often, I turned the machine on with my foot. At these moments, there was no time for finding and pulling on rubber gloves.

I understood that the rules are there to protect the worker and the agency, but hiring someone to look after my son in our home is an entirely different matter. I worked from home and Angus, too, was often present—we were opposed to anything resembling an institutional setting.

❖ ❖ ❖ ❖ ❖

Several weeks earlier, I had explained to the agency that the workers they were sending—non-English-speaking older women (sometimes men) with only elder-care experience—were not right for this placement. Eventually, I complained enough that we negotiated a deal: instead of the agency selecting the staff members that would come to our home, I was permitted to find and interview my own workers, and request that they hire my preferred candidates.

But this wasn't working out either. I was happy I could pick my own support workers but the agency needed to enforce their rules to satisfy their insurance requirements and employment regulations. My favourite rule? Agency caregivers were not allowed to accompany their clients on car rides or take public transit with them without special permission from the agency. Caregivers were permitted to take clients for walks provided they limit the range to the boundaries of the neighbourhood.

The agency could do only so much; I had to go up the chain of command. I called my Community Care Access Centre (CCAC) case manager.

"I don't want the agency any more. I want direct funding. I want to manage the contract myself."

I knew this was a big ask. I expected resistance. To my surprise, I got empathy, understanding, talk of pilot projects, new administration, changes in the air. It was a clear sign that other families had complained too.

"Wonderful! How can I help this move forward? Who do I call? To whom do I address the letter?"

The case manager was accustomed to my cheerful persistence. In some ways I was an easy client—I took control and made specific requests. On the other hand, I challenged and questioned everything.

I knew what was possible. I had heard of others with separate contracts, of individual families that were allowed to manage their own services with direct funding. I was discreet about this information so as not to violate their confidentiality, but it gave me confidence to keep pushing. I wrote the letter, made the calls. I felt like a telemarketer—I had scripted answers to remind myself what to say if they offered up certain arguments. I patiently explained how the current services hadn't accounted for our circumstances, and offered them a way out.

I came to realize that those tasked with meting out the money and services have job descriptions and bosses and lunch breaks and shrinking budgets and quotas and families at home and personal stresses. And all of their clients need more than what they are getting. To be successful, I would need to meet them on their own terms, speak their language and respond to their concerns. It was like a business negotiation.

We reached an equitable agreement. The CCAC gave me an individual contract so I could pay my workers directly and then invoice the government to cover the costs. Which also meant I would stop calling them to negotiate.

Win-win.

# Twenty-one

Michael used to call it the *hum*. A full-body emanation of dry heat. By holding a hand an inch or two from Owen's body you could sense the waves of sickness. Even Owen's knees and ankles would get unusually warm.

I knew we were in for a doozy of an illness. Owen's cough had deepened and he was shaking—probably pneumonia again. It was very early morning and I was in bed, but I hadn't slept at all. Owen had been beside me all night, whimpering, shaking, flinching, also unable to sleep. The thought of a hospital visit at this hour was too much; I needed to get a bit of rest first. Angus was still asleep and I figured this whole thing could wait a couple of hours more. We'd been here before.

I carried Owen out to the living room, settled him in his pillows and went back to bed. Sometimes Owen would actually fall asleep there, in front of the television. Not this morning. He was still shaking when I emerged from my bedroom an hour and a half later. I'd had just enough sleep to ensure I could see straight, and a glass of water to stave off feeling dehydrated and nauseous.

Careful to not jiggle or jostle him, I transferred Owen to his wheelchair. The poor boy probably had a headache on top of all of this. I studied his face carefully—dry mouth, droopy eyelids, down-turned mouth ready to shift from pout to cry, if only he had the energy. He was shaking more intensely—hard enough to make the wheelchair vibrate and slowly turn its wheels, moving him almost imperceptibly across the carpet, as though pushed by a poltergeist.

"Oh boy", I thought. "Here we go". Now, three years later, I look up an old email I sent to Michael:

"I'm taking him to the hospital. He's not his usual sick."

❖ ❖ ❖ ❖ ❖

In all the years since he was released from the hospital as an infant, Owen had never returned to the ICU. On this occasion, however, he was very quickly admitted into intensive care, and swarms of doctors fluttered in and out of the room.

"Stand back," they said.

When the crowds parted, I saw a familiar scene—he had an oxygen mask on his face and several IVs in his hands and feet. The room was very warm; he wore only a diaper.

I rarely observed him from a distance. But this time, as I approached his bed from the other side of the room, I saw him as I imagined others saw him. He'd grown so much! No wonder people asked, "How do you do it?!" He was hardly tall, but lying there quietly, his full body visible, he looked long, almost lanky.

On closer inspection, I noticed that I missed something, something I had never seen before: a funnel had been placed down one nostril, the big open end designed to maximize airflow.

"It's a nasal trumpet. We need to maintain his airway. To avoid a ventilator."

Yes, good idea; although I wanted to rip it out. I had been told many times in recent years:

"Kids like Owen, when they go on the ventilator, have a very hard time coming off . . ." Usually the voice would trail, the sentence dangling incomplete. I didn't have to ask what that meant.

❖ ❖ ❖ ❖ ❖

Owen spent a week in intensive care—enough time for me to learn that intensive care medicine is about one thing only: saving lives. Patching up patients just enough to return to the regular ward where they will deal with healing, medication, bed sores.

Obviously so, you might think. Of course they save lives! How is this at all revealing?

Here's how: If a man is choking and you want to perform the Heimlich manoeuvre, the last thing you might be worried about is breaking a rib, which can happen when you push really hard on someone's torso. It's like that in Intensive Care. They will break your ribs to save your life. And let the wards sort out the resulting non-life-threatening damage.

I learned this during Owen's stay in the ICU. Prior to this illness, we spent months reducing the dose of a benzodiazepine, a sedative, which Owen was taking to help him sleep. Although we were weaning him from this drug to make room for yet another, we were still pleased when we took him off of it completely. Now, the ICU doctor was prescribing a benzodiazepine again.

"Wait. We're not giving that anymore. Our plan is less meds, not more. He'll become addicted."

The doctor remained composed and didn't miss a beat. He looked at me over his glasses.

"Addiction. It's a strong word, no? Has bad connotations, yes?"

Yes! He was dependent on it! That's not good!

He held my gaze steadily, speaking patiently. "If he needs it, he needs it. Instead of addiction, we call it tolerance. If he becomes tolerant, he gets more. If it's too much, he gets less. That's how medicine works."

He scribbled something in the chart and tucked his pen in his shirt pocket.

"You can discuss meds with the other doctors when your son leaves the ICU." He looked at me again, not unkindly. "After we save his life."

❖ ❖ ❖ ❖ ❖

Several days later, Owen lapsed into a deep, un-rousable "somnolent state." For almost 24 hours he did not wake up. The nurses packed him with heat packs as his body temperature plummeted, his breath count dropping to two a minute. In the darkened room, alone with my son and my harrowing thoughts, I swore an oath, "Please Owen, please wake up. Please don't let this be where you draw your last breath. Please don't leave me with this as my memory of our last days together. If you wake up and get better, I will take you home and give you so many better last days. I will make sure you never have to come back."

❖ ❖ ❖ ❖ ❖

Owen was in the hospital for six weeks. When you or I have to stay in the hospital, we can shift ourselves around, turn on the TV, press the call button, ask for water. Owen of course can't do these things; in addition to the nursing staff he required full-time support staff. He also needed advocacy and protection; someone to relay information between nursing shifts, to watch for unusual reactions, to ensure that medications were right and appointments were kept.

I had been living on my own, removed from my suburban bubble, for almost eight months, barely enough to acclimatize to my new life—never mind the crisis unfolding before me. I was juggling my workload and Angus and my own household and personal business. Michael arranged his schedule around work and travel when he could to cover some overnight shifts, but it was I who shouldered the bulk of the responsibility.

I am thankful to have had caregivers, family and friends, and Carsten, my partner of several months, who brought me food, changes of clothes and fresh pillows. He shuttled Angus to and from school, to friends' houses, to the hospital and counselled me gently but firmly to get some sleep on those all-too-infrequent nights off.

❖ ❖ ❖ ❖ ❖

There were many theories circulating as to what might have gone wrong with the baclofen pump. Leaky or dislodged catheter, overdose, kink in the tubing—all tested for and ultimately rejected as probable causes.

After being discharged from intensive care, Owen was placed in a general ward where the patients were recovering from various surgeries. The nurses were focused on the healing of incisions, watching for lingering effects of general anesthetic and documenting the return of regular bodily functions. I sensed that, because Owen's health was so fragile, the physicians on the ward were uncomfortable—they didn't know what was going on and thought that the neurosurgical team should have a better understanding of things.

There was more frustration when, after all the testing, the neurosurgeons didn't have any answers either.

❖ ❖ ❖ ❖ ❖

We were back at the clinic to check on the pump again. The doctor was hesitant. She looked like she was about to say something she would rather not.

"There's been a recall." The words felt like they were entering my brain directly through my forehead. "The pump has a small chamber of gas called propellant. It regulates the pressure inside the medication reservoir. Medtronic has discovered that a very small number of pumps were manufactured without the propellant. They have issued a recall on possible pumps. I have a list of potential serial numbers."

And . . . ?

"And Owen's serial number is on the list."

"I see."

The terms of the recall were different than for, say, a car: this was not an order to remove all suspected pumps and replace them. The surgery is so invasive and the possibility of a faulty pump so low that universal replacement just wouldn't make any sense. Instead, if a serial number was on the list and if there was a problem with the pump evidenced by a number of specific symptoms (of which Owen had some but not all) and if the neurosurgeon determined it was worth investigating, the manufacturer would provide a new replacement pump. Regardless of whether or not Owen was eligible, we were sure that we did not want to replace the pump.

When a pump is removed, it is considered the property of the manufacturer. I briefly considered the idea of applying for a legal injunction to intercept the return delivery of the pump so we could find out independently if anything was wrong with it. But I didn't pursue it.

I didn't really believe it was a pump malfunction and neither did the neurosurgeon. But the recall had an effect on us: it gave us reasonable doubt. And it brought to light just how much faith we were placing in a mechanical device—not just the possibility of improving Owen's quality of life, but the blind trust that it would do no harm. I had only wondered about the effectiveness of the medication, not the quality of the pump itself.

In the end, I settled for the pleasure I felt when we all agreed to titrating the pump dosage down to zero, replacing the pump with saline, and then ultimately removing it. Months after it was taken out, I heard from our doctor that the manufacturer did not find anything wrong with it. I wouldn't have been surprised either way.

❖ ❖ ❖ ❖ ❖

The intrathecal baclofen pump came out 18 months after it was initially inserted. The procedures left a long, re-opened scar on Owen's belly and a sunken space where the device had been. A small patch of puffy skin remained which seemed to have trapped some extra fluid. The scar on Owen's back was less noticeable, but I could still feel a sinewy thread of tissue growth where the catheter had been. I would sometimes place my hand over his belly, completely covering the scar, and try to remember what he looked like without it.

# Twenty-two

Owen attended Sunny View Public School from October 15, 07 until March 17, 08, when he became affected by respiratory difficulties and problems with his Baclofen pump, resulting in increased muscle tone and has not returned to school since. Owen is now receiving his education from the Home Schooling program through the TDSB.

**Speech-Language Pathology Report, Toronto District School Board, June 10, 2008**

I kept my promise to Owen; when he came home from the hospital I made the call to Sunny View and told them that Owen was not coming back.

I had been interviewing new support workers just before Owen became sick. All except one were deaf. I emailed or texted them to let them know interviews and decisions were being suspended until Owen got better and that I couldn't be sure when that would be.

Now at home and without a schooling program, I didn't have enough support for Owen; I had to hire someone, quickly. I thought about the six or seven people who had applied and wondered who I should contact first. Really, there was only one good candidate. I rifled through the resumes until I found the one I was looking for: Sallyanne. Hard of hearing CODA (Child of Deaf Adults). Fluent in ASL and can talk on the phone. Experience? Summer camp with kids with disabilities, *blah blah blah* . . . Didn't matter; she was qualified enough. But most importantly, she could hear. I knew I could explain things quickly and that she would hear when Owen choked. She's the one.

When I first started hiring support, I would ask primarily about experience. "Have you ever worked in a group home before?"

I would sometimes be interested in education and future goals. "How did you decide to get into nursing? Where would you like to be in 5 years?"

Over time, I shifted focus to disability awareness and attitude. "Suppose children in the playground were staring at Owen. What would you say to them?"

I became a great interviewer. Unfortunately the quality of the answers usually had no bearing on whether or not the person would work out.

I learned to develop my internal radar: How would I feel having this person in my home? Does she wear perfume or smoke? Do I like how he talks? Does she look sturdy enough to lift Owen off the floor? Does he grate on my nerves?

The regular interview questions were just a way to tease out personality, perspective, intelligence, kindness. There was usually only one relevant question to which I needed an honest answer: "Are you comfortable cleaning up bodily fluids?"

Kind, intelligent, patient, creative, not easily grossed out. All the rest can be taught.

Sallyanne was a quick study. She was nervous at first but quickly became confident and skilled. Nothing scared her—day trips, swimming, camps, public transit. She was a full-time support for Owen and a godsend for me. I tried to contain my disappointment when she told me, "I'm pregnant."

She helped me interview her replacements, taking the new trainees to Toronto Island for the day to "break them in." Sallyanne was being replaced by several new helpers who would work shorter shifts. We agreed that Owen was too much work for one person, eight hours a day. And because Sallyanne was full-time, I held my breath every day hoping she wouldn't call in sick.

With the new arrangement, I could be assured on any given day that someone would eventually come, regardless of cars not starting, bouts of the flu and too much snow.

❖ ❖ ❖ ❖ ❖

Sallyanne's tenure with us marked the beginning of a new phase for Owen (and Angus and me). I hired based solely on heart and willingness to learn—and it was a huge success. During the last year of Owen's life he had six support workers with different strengths and interests. Jamie baked, made crafts—and she came with us on daytrips and holidays. Mark took Owen swimming every week; Daina enjoyed books and movies with Owen; Bethany took Owen on long walks and trips to Starbucks; Marjorie engaged in stimulating play; for some reason, Owen napped frequently with Ashley—they spent much of her shift cuddled in the "big chair." And all of them absorbed Angus into the fold as though he were their own.

I didn't have to find them all myself; current workers referred their own friends, family members and acquaintances . . . eventually, all of Owen's caregivers came to know each other, sometimes socializing outside of duty hours and sometimes even meeting each other while working with Owen. A true community.

I held a Caregivers Christmas party in 2009, the year before Owen died, and invited caregivers old and new, spouses, kids. A rollicking time with Secret Santa, charades, potluck food and too many sweets. It was the one time I didn't need to hire someone specifically for the event; the caregivers took turns helping out. After Owen died I still held the Christmas party.

# Twenty-three

Deep brain stimulation (DBS) is exactly how it sounds, but worse. A probe is guided down through the centre of a hole drilled at the top of the head and permanently placed more or less where the misfires in the brain are occurring. I say "more or less" because, more likely than not, the neurosurgeons can only guess at where the misfiring occurs. The lead to the probe, a very thin wire, is then laid flat against the skull under the scalp; an incision bisecting that half of the head is made in order to insert the wire. The lead winds its way down along the side of the head, down the neck to connect with its battery source, tucked under the collarbone. When it is implanted in children some slack is left in the line to account for growth and movement. The battery is charged every night through a wireless connection to the charger located in a holster, worn over the shoulder.

❖ ❖ ❖ ❖ ❖

DBS had, as an option for Owen, been on the horizon for many months; years, even. Especially with the failure of the intrathecal baclofen pump, it was the next (and only) option to try to rein in the dystonia that was causing his uncomfortable wayward movements.

If Owen suffered only uncontrollable motion and random movement, things might have been manageable without considering further intervention. However, his spasticity and dystonia were throwing his whole body out of whack. He was developing contractures in his knees, and one hip was well on its way to complete dislocation from the constant tension and twisting of his torso and legs. It was increasingly challenging to lift, hold and transfer him in and out of his wheelchair.

I resisted DBS. I was repulsed. I thought, just because we can do a thing doesn't mean we should. And we had only recently emerged from the failed experiment of the other implanted device, the sting of regret still with me. I was like a fussy child, hands on ears repeating No! No! No! What was I so afraid of? Was it not my job—my duty—to know the thing I was so roundly rejecting? At some point I decided it was time to be an adult, to trust that I could still make the right decision in the face of dwindling options, exuberant studies and videos of miracles on YouTube.

I wondered often how a parent separates personal motivations from the needs of the child. What are my own motivations for making decisions? Could it be an inability to accept my own helplessness? Is it my own lack of discernment that sends me pursuing any and all available options? What is a reasonable level of pain and discomfort that I should allow to be visited upon my helpless and vulnerable son? How do I distinguish between acting out of compassion and indulging my ego?

❖ ❖ ❖ ❖ ❖

Angus. I watch as Angus grows and notice that occasionally I must step back, step away, to allow him to experience crushing disappointment, heartbreak, loss, the natural consequences of a bad decision. I can sit by him but cannot fix it all—often because I'm not able to, but also because it's my duty as his mother to prepare him for what lies ahead.

And then there's Owen. What lay ahead for him? What in the world was I preparing him for? I knew one thing that was coming for sure: a bigger body that would be harder to manage. Owen had already burned through caregivers at a rate that made me reconsider the entire support structure, replacing one full-time caregiver with six who were part-time. But what to do about it? Soon, he would be un-liftable by one person—possibly even un-carryable. Soon, he would need a much larger shower stall with a much larger mesh chair. Soon, he would need a ceiling lift and a bigger wheelchair and adult diapers. Soon, we would have to move to a bigger place to accommodate all the stuff.

Those things didn't scare me. The logistics could be figured out. The equipment could be made-to-measure and ordered. A new home could be arranged. But in Owen's case, *bigger* generally meant increasing tightness, increasing discomfort, increasing difficulty in transferring him from location to location, more opportunities to be dropped or get stuck.

Physical calmness would be an important part of a peaceful adulthood for him and for everyone around him. Medications, surgery and physiotherapy are the traditional means to accomplish this, none of which had done Owen much good. Medications were generally maxed out—he had some room to increase the dose on a couple of them, but not much. There were no other surgeries on offer that would have relieved anything and we had stopped formal physiotherapy a long time ago.

And what of alternative medicines and treatments? In theory, there are many interesting—possibly good—ideas floating around. In reality, nothing helped. Herbs, minerals, energy work, alternative therapies, Traditional Chinese Medicine. ("Go like this!" The practitioner of Chinese medicine, who was also an MD, shook Owen's limbs, lightly slapped his forearms. "Give him more vigour!")

To be fair, I admit I didn't stick with any treatment long enough to determine its benefits. Owen's condition was severe—I called it "chronically acute"—a situation difficult to treat with remedies. We encountered (and tried) expensive, unregulated and unproven offerings whose effects were often too subtle to determine what, if anything, was happening. The world of alternative treatments is a minefield of hucksters and charlatans, making it difficult to separate the legitimate claims from the shams.

I have a theory: many alternative therapies and medicines are helpful because patients feel they are being seen, heard, understood. Because of the level at which they are engaged, patients feel they are active participants in their own care and feel less vulnerable, more in charge of their own health. There is an important connection between patient and practitioner that I suspect goes a long way towards improving health, regardless of the biochemical efficacy of the intervention.

Sceptics might call this a classic placebo effect. And of course, Owen was immune. He never convinced himself (or me) that something was working when it wasn't.

If there was an alternative option that was going to ease any of his symptoms, we hadn't encountered it yet.

So, by all measures, DBS was an option to consider. Despite my negative reaction to such an invasive course of action, I wondered if it wasn't perhaps less invasive than all of those medications I was giving him 4 times a day. Baclofen, clonazepam, tizanidine, valproic acid . . . Surely, a "simple" device could trump all those meds, each of which had its own side effects and risks.

I was haunted by the idea that my own emotionally based resistance, not yet under the microscope or subject to scrutiny, was the only thing in the way of a potentially life-changing and fabulous intervention. I wondered in my blog: how silly will I feel five or ten years from now, when this practice is commonplace and successful? Perhaps I'm the one who needs an intervention.

❖ ❖ ❖ ❖ ❖

Intervention came in the person of a lawyer, who was also a bioethicist at Bloorview. I found Maria McDonald through the institutional connections I made within the meandering social network into which I wandered seeking professional advice. She agreed to speak with me and see if she could help shed some light on my quandary.

We talked at length about disability, decisions, how one approaches such a thing. It was interesting, if also a little awkward—I'd prepared little for our conversation and felt we were having a kind of student-teacher chit-chat at a college luncheon.

About twenty minutes into our meeting I realized I was biding my time—waiting for her to stand up and say, "On behalf of disabled children and righteous good ethics everywhere, I decree that you shall . . ." and would then pronounce the just and upright thing to do.

Of course, she didn't. She kept the conversation balanced and thoughtful and if she had a specific opinion, I don't think she expressed it. Most of her side of the conversation was aimed at explaining the role of an ethics committee, Ontario and Canadian law and hospital rules of conduct.

Fascinating—but not immediately helpful. Or maybe I should say, it was only helpful to the extent that it reaffirmed that it was I alone who had to make these decisions on behalf of Owen, and regardless of how unprepared I felt, I was legally equipped to do so. I couldn't relinquish this decision to an ethicist, a surgeon, a clinic, some research report or the Internet. I would need to sort it out for myself, and with Michael. What a weighty responsibility.

I suspect I had fallen into the same trap as many other parents; well intentioned and loving as we are, we fail to see beyond the physical or tangible pros and cons of a procedure or a surgery. To soothe the anxiety of uncertainty, it is easier to want to take refuge in statistics and information—maybe Google will provide the answer. But all that research can increase the opportunity and intensity of confusion. Will it help? Is it risky? Have others benefited? Have others died? These questions are all likely to be answered in the affirmative. So, then what? The calculation of risk doesn't matter if your child turns out to be the one who died, or the one who lived, or the one who could walk. What matters is what formed the basis of the decision in the first place.

I realized that decisions like this must be cast in a different light—not only because of the seriousness of the intervention or the potential risks, but because guardians of vulnerable people who can't speak for themselves must hold themselves to a higher standard—to higher principles that embrace the humanity in all those concerned.

Some questions I struggled to answer:
- What would I do if I were in Owen's situation?
- What would I do if I were deciding for myself?
- What do I think he would decide for himself?

It didn't help that each of these answers was different.

Then more questions:
- What level of risk can reasonably be assigned to someone else who has no say in the matter and who doesn't know there is a choice to be made?
- Given that this decision must be made on behalf of someone else, do I have the right to say yes?
- Given that this decision must be made on behalf of someone else, do I have the right to say no?

In this particular case, Owen's manageability is linked directly to his quality of life. If Owen's body were more manageable, he would be easier to connect with, easier to bring into the community, easier to support at home.

❖ ❖ ❖ ❖ ❖

I booked an appointment for Michael and me to discuss the deep brain stimulation procedure with the neurologists and neurosurgeons at Toronto Western General Hospital, who specialize in DBS. Successfully used to treat depression, dystonia and Parkinson's in adults, it is now finding its way into severely disabled children with dystonia. (The battery pack is now small enough to fit into child-sized bodies.) The procedure was only conducted at this hospital, not at Sick Kids; most of the patients so far had been adults.

I was looking forward to exploring the possibilities and finding out more and hoping to rule this option out or in. Despite my resistance to agreeing to another potentially unhelpful surgically implanted device, I was committed to continuing the dialogue until a decision had to be made. I was still anticipating the moment at which all that research would turn into an obvious answer.

I learned that, at the time of our meeting, only a handful of children in Canada similar to Owen had had the procedure done, and only a few of them had had the device implanted long enough to report any results—most without improvement or with minimal improvement.

Interestingly, the neurologist cited official-sounding statistics, like "1 to 2% will experience a stroke during the procedure due to burst blood vessels". One to two percent? Based on a sample of fewer than ten? I asked for clarification. The number was extrapolated from the adult population and applied to what they know about children's brains. Fair enough. But to me, the explanation rendered the numbers virtually meaningless.

We discussed the ins and outs, the pros and cons, the ups and downs. Random comments from the team:

"Maybe it will help. Maybe not."

"May provide some pain relief. Maybe not."

"May cause tingles or additional posturing. Maybe not."

"Probably can't hurt. Maybe."

"If you've tried everything else, I can't see a reason not to try this."

"As far as brain surgery goes, this is pretty low risk."

"No, we won't take it out if it doesn't work. But it might be worth a try."

"Why not?"

❖ ❖ ❖ ❖ ❖

I knew before the meeting was over that we wouldn't pursue it. Michael had already made his preference clear: no more surgeries. In my own mind I had dismissed this as too simplistic an answer, but I was coming around to his way of thinking. The very nature of the meeting, another instance of the pattern I had seen time and again, had put me off.

When a patient has a complex or mysterious problem, the path of referral goes something like this: see a generalist; get referred to a specialist who knows the condition; get further referred to a sub-specialist who does the operation for that condition. The scope of the problem and skill set of the practitioner become increasingly specialized the closer you get to the end of the referral chain, like being funnelled through narrower and narrower pathways. The path of referral to any particular specialist can take many months, and sometimes years—the legitimacy of the path itself is not called into question at this point. The specialist assumes you've done your research and you, the patient or parent, are happy to have finally found someone with a solution. Following this path, the journey can feel like a single, inevitable trail leading to a grand, final conclusion.

With blinders on and a narrow focus, it is hard to see the full picture: the medical system is, in fact, a complex maze that could shoot an unwitting participant down any one of many dark tunnels that may end in any one of many possible chambers. Which chamber you end up in can be highly contingent on who you saw last; what they knew; what they read; how they choose to curate, editorialize and distil the information at their disposal.

I have heard some parents complain about physicians. About lack of compassion, about poor bedside manner, about unfortunate uses of certain words and terminology, about pessimistic prognoses. I have occasionally experienced some of these things, but I have no such complaints. I imagine that some medical specialties attract certain personality types—they are more like engineers or technologists or research scientists than they are like therapists or healers or counsellors. To do what they do, they must be detached, curious, intellectual. And willing to fail. Naturally, it is reasonable to expect clarity, courtesy and civility. But for me, anything beyond that is a bonus.

Specialists often function in communities resembling special interest groups. They have their own funding, their own agendas, their own perspectives. Perhaps they are seeking to prove a thesis; perhaps they hold a noble vision of advancing the profession, adding to a collective body of knowledge. They may be looking to develop an idea that has been years, decades, in the making. A clinician may be trying to determine whether your case fits with what they have to offer. They are assessing to see if you are a good candidate and whether or not you and they are likely to experience a successful outcome.

The problem lies not with this agenda. The problem is how a patient interprets it. If my son fits the profile and they say, "Yes, we can do it," it's tempting to assume that whatever they're offering is the right solution. Finer minds than my own have spent a lot of time and money focusing on this one specialty, and thank goodness for that: they solve mysteries, improve chances, save lives.

But the specialist doesn't have the time or inclination or even perspective to reflectively delineate the scope of his or her special interest. They simply do what they do.

❖ ❖ ❖ ❖ ❖

The neurologist looked Owen up and down, thinking out loud. She recited a high-level checklist, crossing each item off one by one. Fixed postures? No. Is he big enough? Yes. Parents understand the surgical risks? Yes.

"Well then. We can try."

Yes, of course we can try. And it was good to know that DBS was an option. But our answer was no.

❖ ❖ ❖ ❖ ❖

I left that appointment practically skipping. I felt I had passed a test, or resisted a strong temptation. Not because we decided against the surgery but because I knew we had reached the best decision for Owen, given everything we knew and all we had experienced, in spite of the forces moving us in a different direction. We decided that there would be no more surgeries, no more implants, no more invasive procedures.

With this one decision, I enjoyed a surprising new freedom. There was nothing left to hold out for, no more straws at which to grasp, no more hope for improvement, no theories to explore, no further experiments, no more trials. Finally, Owen was free to just be. I have no doubt he felt just as much relief as I did.

# Twenty-four

The body is that of a boy, 4'2" in length and 56 lb in weight.
    a. The body build is small and thin.
    b. The skin is clean.
The body is clothed: orange long-sleeved T-shirt; diaper; blue socks. The body is lying on a plaid comforter.

**Report of Postmortem Examination, October 24, 2010**

I saw his name on the phone display and wondered why Michael would be calling me at, what . . . 8:30 on a Sunday morning? He probably wants me to pick the boys up early. I bristled slightly, bracing myself for the disappointment of a shortened weekend. Crap. Oh well. I picked up the phone.

I answered in the manner one does knowing who is on the other end. A "Hey-lo" and an expectant pause. There wasn't an immediate reply. Instead there was silence, and then wheezy breathing. I smiled.

It was an old joke of Michael's and mine to put Owen on the phone. Whoever was with Owen would say "Hold on! Someone wants to talk to you," then hold the phone receiver up to Owen's mouth and let him breathe into it. Owen found this infinitely funny and would start to laugh. (This little charade was all the more funny because Owen was deaf! I like to imagine Owen found this even funnier than we did.) His laugh almost always started with a suspension of breath, followed by a chuckling or wheezing sound, followed by a gasping in-breath. He would then continue to breathe/laugh into the receiver, sounding like Darth Vader. A fuzzy, static-y sound that was instantly recognizable to Michael and me. The other would say "Hi Bubby!" and politely wait for the joke to be over.

I heard the pause—a silent beat—then the wheeze. Silly Michael and Owen. I was amused, rolling my eyes good-naturedly. But still, it's Sunday morning and if there's a change of plans, well then, let's get on with it.

"Hi Owen! What are you guys up to?" I knew Michael could hear me.

Another wheeze, then, "No, it's me. Michael."

Wait. Is he laughing? No, he's crying. Gasping for breath himself. I felt a swirling sensation, a pressure at the centre of the back of my head.

He said it quietly, slightly high-pitched: "Owen passed away last night."

What? "Are you joking?" I don't know why I said it because I knew it was true.

No, it's true, just please come. I hung up and looked at Carsten, dazed. He seemed to already know. He left to put on his shoes and fetch the car.

❖ ❖ ❖ ❖ ❖

I had been thinking about this moment for months, years. When Owen dies, what do I do? Owen's environment and experiences were so controlled I had imagined a specific sort of death. I assumed it would happen when he was with me, in my house, possibly in my bed and in my arms. I would wake from a night of cradling him in our customary position and I would find that he had died in the night. In this event, I was told by our doctor, I would not need to call emergency services. I could put him in a respectful position on his bed and call a doctor to come, who would pronounce his death and help take care of details. No need for ambulances, chaos, autopsies.

❖ ❖ ❖ ❖ ❖

We rode up the elevator in silence. I didn't ask any questions. On any other day I would have noticed the ambulance and police car in front of the building. But it wasn't any other day, and I didn't.

Michael led me into the little nook where Owen usually slept—the condo version of the modern day den or home office (or third bedroom if you have a small body, few belongings and an active imagination). It was a tiny, separate space between the kitchen and living room. It had a picture window and was just big enough for a toddler bed and a wooden hutch. Everything was Owen-size.

Owen was on the bed, on his back, face and body covered with the red blanket I bought when he was an infant—red is good for the root chakra, a friend had said. The fluffy tuft of hair at the top of his head just visible under the tangled fringe of the cover. I took in the scene slowly, as though my brain was filming in slow motion. I felt the presence of uniformed strangers behind me, keeping a respectful distance.

I knelt down beside the little bed. Yes, I thought, yes, this is he. This is my son. It has happened. I held my head in my hands. And I wept.

# Twenty-five

Angus was Owen's champion, his pal, his biggest fan. Would he have developed self-consciousness about Owen? Would he ever have become embarrassed? He was ten when his brother died and it hadn't happened yet. Friends had warned of it, yet there has never been a whiff of it.

Angus stroked his hair, held his hand, soothed him, entertained him, sought comfort from him; never shied away from introducing Owen to his friends, held his wheelchair when walking down the street, engaging with Owen on Owen's own terms.

Angus rarely cried before Owen died. He cried even less in the months following Owen's death, until the dam broke and the emotions started to surface.

Sometimes at night, Angus weeps. At first I tried to comfort him but it was awkward, hard to get close. I was ordered away.

We eventually tacitly agreed on a system. Now when Angus is sad, I sit at the foot of his bed on the beanbag chair I bought Owen for his last birthday, pretending to write but really just listening to Angus. (Angus insists the chair will accompany him when he moves out.) I coach myself through this most challenging of parenting trials. Let him be, I think. Don't interrupt.

I wait for an open moment and give him a tissue or a glass of water. As I sit and listen and peck at the keyboard my heart breaks for my remaining son who must now live out his days without his brother. Sometimes, after the tears, he will say, "I wish he didn't die."

❖ ❖ ❖ ❖ ❖

I think about Angus becoming a teenager, then a young man, with all of this behind him. He will travel, meet people, date. I think about him moving away, going to college, getting a job, falling in love. How will he carry this? How will this loss shape his relationships, his life?

Maybe his partners won't know right away. Maybe he will hold his brother close to his chest until the time is right. Maybe he will wait until trust is earned and hearts are connected. Sometime between the initial crush and his commitment of undying love, maybe he will say, "I want to tell you about my brother."

# Acknowledgements

To those who provided skilful advice in the preparation of this book and those whose expertise and guidance gave me what I needed to make difficult decisions; I offer my heartfelt gratitude and appreciation:

First and foremost to S.K. Johannesen—my father and writing mentor, my critic and inspiration; to Carsten Knoch—my greatest supporter, partner and best friend, whose encouragement and faith made this book a reality. To my whole family, especially: my mother Yippy Novotny; my friend and step-mother Penny Winspur; my brother Ben Johannesen—who were close to this project from the beginning. And to my dear friends who cheered me on, in particular: Jane Salter, Vivien Carrady, Deirdre Walsh and Mariellen Ward.

To Dr. Golda Milo-Manson of Holland Bloorview Kids Rehabilitation Hospital, Owen's pediatric specialist for almost 10 years. Much more than "just" a doctor to us, she felt our disappointments and successes right along with us. Dr. Greg Ryan and Dr. Rory Windrim of Mount Sinai Hospital, who set the highest bar for patient interaction and treatment. The Hospital for Sick Children (Toronto) Neurology and Neurosurgery departments, especially Dr. Brenda Banwell, Lynn MacMillan and Dr. Jim Drake, for their expertise in treating Owen and dedication to solving his mysteries.

To the Low to the Ground Publishing family, including David London, Natalia Pérez Wahlberg, Chuck Finkle and Dean Macdonell, for their commitment to quality in producing this book.

To Owen's caregivers of the last two years: Sallyanne Hadzalic, Jamie Seguin, Daina Sutton, Mark Hardy, Bethany Hardy, Ashley Ellinor, Indiana Acuna, Marjorie Richards and Jessica Cano-Jauregui.

Finally, to Michael Turney, who has shared this journey with me from the beginning. I wish to emphasize this: his deep connection with Owen, his commitment to his role as his father and his active participation in decision-making are grossly underrepresented in these pages. If he were so inclined to write a book, he would have a remarkable story of his own to tell.

CPSIA information can be obtained at www.ICGtesting.com
Printed in the USA
LVOW12s2140020614

388234LV00006B/10/P